I Don't Need You When I'm Right

I Don't Need You When I'm Right

THE CONFESSIONS OF A WASHINGTON PR MAN

by Vic Gold

WILLIAM MORROW & COMPANY, INC.
NEW YORK   1975

Library of Congress Cataloging in Publication Data

Gold, Vic.
    I don't need you when I'm right.

1. Public relations consultants—United States—
Correspondence, reminiscences, etc.   2. Gold, Vic.
3. Public relations and politics.   I. Title.
HM263.G57   659.2'329'00924 [B]   74-34270
ISBN 0-688-02909-4

Book design by Helen Roberts

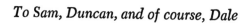

To Sam, Duncan, and of course, Dale

Contents

"*I'm with you when you're right, Governor. But not when you're wrong.*"

"*You stupid sonofabitch. I don't need you when I'm right!*"

Earl Long Stories A. J. Liebling missed (From the Private Vintage Collection of David M. Kleck, New Orleans, Louisiana)

1. Tell 'Em the Truth: Tell 'Em I Lied

It looks like we have a little PR problem.

Jeb Magruder, breaking the news on Watergate to
Bob Mardian

I arrived in Washington, D.C., on the subfreezing morning of December 1, 1958, with a family of two, twins
on the way, the promise of a $7,500 a year job with a
public relations agency, and the consuming ambition to
become press secretary to a President of the United
States. Damned near made it, too, but luck was with me.
Jim Hagerty, Pierre Salinger, George Reedy, Ron Ziegler,
Jerry terHorst . . . where are they now?

Where *I* am—after fifteen years of working Pennsylvania Avenue from Capitol Hill to one-heartbeat-and-
a-press-release away from the White House—is what this
book is about.

But first, let me put my own house in order. A Washington press agent who sets out to write a candid book
about power, politics, and PR owes it to his conscience,

his readers, and his potential victims to begin by breaking his own cover stories. Let me explain.

There are three secrets I have carefully concealed throughout my career in Washington, personal information known only to my wife and the special agent of the Federal Bureau of Investigation assigned to compile my dossier when Lyndon Johnson checked me out during the 1964 Presidential campaign.

First, I was born in East St. Louis, Illinois, *not* New Orleans, Louisiana, as I claimed in my application to Burning Tree Country Club.

Second, I voted for John F. Kennedy in 1960, not Richard M. Nixon because—so help me Bill Buckley— I actually thought at the time that any son of Joe Kennedy had to be more conservative than a running mate of Henry Cabot Lodge.

Third, I drink Chivas Regal Scotch, not Old Fitzgerald Bourbon. On the rocks.

Being passed over by Burning Tree is no great loss, but the second and third confessions will come as something of a shock to at least three of my former employer-clients: Spiro Agnew, Barry Goldwater, and going back to my days as an independent PR counsel, the Bourbon Institute. Senator Goldwater, a bourbon man, might even be offended on two counts.

But the truth must come out because, though born in East St. Louis, I spent my formative years in the political ambience of Earl Long's Louisiana, where candor is an accepted political attribute; not because the politicians of Lousiana are virtuous but because, given the state's political past, the threshhold for popular shock is higher there than in the other forty-nine states.

In fact, my earliest recollection of politics was that of Louisiana Governor Richard Leche going to the penitentiary for candor-in-avarice. ("When I took the oath of office, I didn't take any vows of poverty.") He was joined there, in short order, by a large retinue of friends and supporters, an inspiring demonstration of excessive political loyalty.

It was a lesson, fortunately, that didn't escape the notice of an eleven-year-old East St. Louis transplant on-the-make. Because even then the urge to get involved in the power-and-politics game was strong, my specific goal being to help the new governor, Earl Long, extricate the state from the coils of corruption.

Some years later, as a law student at the University of Alabama, I found that my urge was endemic to the region's youth. Two out of five of my classmates wanted to be Governor of Alabama. The other three were working to become powers behind the throne.

The roles are complementary but conflicting, as I learned in my later dealings with candidates and PR clients. Some seekers after power grab for the brass ring. Others, because of short reach or fear of falling off the merry-go-round, are willing to settle for giving advice on how to grab it and, if successful, to fondle it a little now and then.

There are ego problems here, complications I'll go into later. For now it's enough to say that the political candidate—a man who thinks of himself as the salvation of millions—is possessed of a unique super-ego. But the PR counsel—a man who thinks he can manipulate that kind of super-ego—suffers from even greater delusions. Like Henry VIII's Cardinal Wolsey, the manipulator, if he presses his luck too far, is bound to end in a ditch somewhere muttering imprecations against princes or Presidents.

Such problems were in the distant future, however,

and didn't concern me while I attended law classes at the University of Alabama during the day and earned my keep as a political press agent at night.

My first major move into politics came during the Alabama Democratic primary of 1950. I was appointed campus chairman for Gordon Persons, a liberal candidate in the governor's race. Oh yes, I was a liberal then, which by standards of the time and place meant being *against* child labor and *for* the forty-cent minimum wage. I also came out in favor of Louis Armstrong appearing on campus, which marked me as something of an ultra. But none of this had anything to do with the debacle that followed.

They appointed me on Monday. On Tuesday they learned I was Jewish.

If you think being born in East St. Louis would be bad on the status at Burning Tree, you should have seen how they reacted to the idea of a Jewish campaign chairman in Alabama in 1950. I was there before Eagleton.

Why hadn't I told anybody?

Told them what?

That you were . . . that you were . . .

They offered me a face-saver. I could work in the finance office. After all, there's always a place for a nice Jewish boy in a finance office—even in Alabama in 1950.

I told them I didn't know anything about finance.

Impossible. *All* Jewish boys know something about finance. It's like black people and the rhythm thing.

But they were finally convinced, and deciding that I could *write*, they ended up stashing me in a back room to grind out speeches and press releases for various WASP front men they called co-chairmen to cover up the goof.

Our candidate took the state in a landslide. But more

4

important, he won the campus straw poll taken three days before the election. I was on my way. Of course, I really didn't expect an invitation to the Inaugural . . .

All of which may have had something to do with a later distaste for politicians who call themselves liberal.

There was another young politician they told me was liberal, back during those early Alabama years: an ambitious legislator from South Alabama named George Wallace. I finally got a chance to meet George four years later, when he was one of Big Jim Folsom's campaign managers in the 1954 Alabama governor's race and I was trying to convince Folsom he needed the help of a professional PR man.

Big Jim—"Kissin' Jim," as he was called elsewhere in the country—was at the zenith of his political career that year, headed for a landslide victory and a second term as governor. It didn't trouble me at all that a big item in the Folsom campaign was attacking the outgoing governor, my candidate four years before.

A Southern populist whose political strength lay in his gigantesque 6-foot 8-inch appeal to Alabama's rustic majority, Folsom gathered around him most of Alabama's youngest, hungriest, shrewdest politicians. Wallace, a state circuit judge—they called him "the Little Judge"—was one of this upwardly mobile group.

The 1954 Democratic primary for all practical purposes elected the governor, since the state's Republican party was then still in a post-Reconstruction coma. That particular primary occurred a month before the historic Supreme Court desegregation decision in *Brown* v. *Board of Education of Topeka.* The politics of segregation— "seg," as it came to be known during the next ten years —played no significant role in the campaign. What nonwhite votes were cast went Folsom's way since he, too, was considered a liberal by regional standards.

Despite my youth, friends in Montgomery touted me to Big Jim as the sharpest political PR man in the state. But that was an era when nobody under thirty could expect to be taken seriously by old pro politicians.

Wallace, however, was a young pro. Though what I had to offer fell on deaf ears in most of the Folsom camp, "the Little Judge" proved receptive to one idea I was trying to sell: using television to help overcome the Alabama print media's hostility to Folsom's candidacy. It was a PR case problem—and proposed solution—that would recur a decade and a half later when I worked for candidates playing for higher stakes.

The problem: Big Jim was attracting large crowds, but the state's major newspapers were down-playing his day-to-day campaign. Like Lyndon Johnson and other Y'all Come-type candidates brought up in the press-the-flesh school of politics, Folsom wasn't at home in a television studio. His free-swinging country boy-style didn't come through the cathodes, and he knew it. As a result, Folsom usually prepared for TV speeches with massive doses of Kentucky's finest. It was a habit that tended to give his studio appearances what audio-visual experts now call an "uneven quality."

Yet television in the 1950s had already become a fact of political life that even a rustic candidate couldn't ignore. What I proposed is old wool hat now, but it was novel at the time: if you can't bring the country boy to the studio, take the studio to the country boy. I offered to produce a film of Folsom rallies, so that TV audiences could see the candidate in his own corn bread milieu. But my suggested price for the project was considered outlandish by Folsom's old-line country boy advisers, whose idea of PR budgeting was limited to the cost of buying telephone pole placards and car windshield stickers.

Wallace, however, liked the film idea and picked it up. He put together a single half-hour television package of Folsom rally film clips and arranged to have it shown election eve on major stations around the state.

What impact the film had on the outcome of the Alabama gubernatorial primary of 1954 is speculative at best, since Folsom won it, going away. The rule is that in a close election a winning candidate may concede that outside PR counsel had something to do with his victory. But never in a landslide. The candidate who wins big doesn't need anybody. He knows he's a political genius who did it all on his own.

It figured that in the heady aftermath of his landslide, Big Jim couldn't have been less interested in any proposal to put a Birmingham city slicker PR consultant on his payroll. What's more, he was amazed that I'd even be *interested* in such a job, though not because he thought I belonged in the finance office.

No, what baffled Big Jim was that a lawyer—I had earned my degree by that time—would want to lower himself to *press* work. He was mystified, because as a layman he considered a law degree a license to steal. And as a politician of candor, on the order of my early Louisiana mentors, he told audiences as much.

"Why is it," he asked plaintively when his administration fell into the coils, "that when *I* take it they call it stealing. But when a *lawyer* governor takes it, they call it a fee?"

So the governor turned my talents away, and with lines like that, I couldn't much blame him. My friends in court at Montgomery claimed I was the best PR man in the state. No, Big Jim argued, he can't be.

7

"If he's the best PR man in Alabama," said Folsom, "then how come I'm governor and he's not?"

For me, the politics of candor translated into a press agentry of candor. But at times the virtue lost something in translation. Take those occasions when I had to carry unpleasant news to a client. Say, that he was going to lose a campaign. Or that Scotch sales were up for the quarter, and I, personally, had done nothing to discourage the trend.

It was only after coming to Washington that I learned the art of euphemism is the better part of public relations.

Working with the Bourbon Institute, for example, I had a special problem. I was fond of Bill Marshall, the Institute president. But my doctor told me I was allergic to bourbon. It gave me headaches. I knew that was ridiculous—that bourbon doesn't give people headaches any more than Scotch or vodka or gin do. I knew it because I hadn't simply *read* the Bourbon Institute material on the subject, I'd *written* it. But the fact was—call it the crossing of Scorpio and Aries or my Bio-curve of the moment—every time I downed a bourbon, I woke up the following morning *thinking* I had a headache.

Naturally, I couldn't let my client know. So I skirted the issue. I kept talking about how much my *wife* liked bourbon (which was true). That, and avoiding cocktail parties attended by Institute members, helped me keep the account until I went to work for a Vice President of the United States who drank Chivas Regal Scotch, with soda and no excuses.

But before learning the art of euphemism, a penchant for candor often got me into trouble with PR clients back in Alabama.

In my first year as a lawyer-political consultant in

Birmingham, I had a young maverick candidate for mayor named Arthur Parker. He was a frustrated Shakespearean actor—most working politicians are frustrated something-or-others—and his forte was speaking above people's heads. This was fine with me because I was on an Adlai Stevenson kick at the time.

Within days, I had Parker talking about Birmingham transit and garbage problems at a forensic level more suitable to plenary sessions of the UN General Assembly, circa 1953. The speeches went over like lead balloons in Birmingham's steel mill precincts, but it was good practice for a future Washington speech hack (though not particularly useful, as we'll see, in writing speeches for Jerry Ford).

Parker went into the campaign on a lark, backed by half a dozen mavericks just out of law school. We were doing fine, what with me writing inspirational speeches and him delivering them with Shakespearean élan to a bemused but friendly local press. We had no expectation of winning; it was only good, clean fun at City Hall expense.

Then one day late in the campaign Parker suddenly began taking the whole thing seriously. He asked me if I thought he had a chance to win.

"Not a whore's prayer," I answered, rolling speech copy through the typewriter. Twenty years later—specifically, after a succession of defeats from governorships to Senate seats to the Presidency—I would have handled it differently. Not lying, of course; just the varnished truth. With experience I learned ways of handling such situations candidly, yet without losing the candidate's confidence.

There is, for example, the art of silent euphemism—the knowing wink or elbow in the ribs—popular in political backrooms. But if the candidate keeps pressing and you have to talk, there are other ways: you can tell him that it's too bad, but he's ahead of his time. Or that he's really too honest to get elected. Or that even if he wins the election the bastards down at City Hall will probably steal it.

None of which I did in answering Arthur Parker that afternoon in the spring of 1953, which, I guess, was why my candidate didn't ask me anything else the rest of the campaign. Not even to draft his concession statement.

But the Parker campaign was only the beginning of my transition from law to full-time public relations. From 1953 through the spring of 1958 I found myself involved in a series of campaigns, from tax assessor to governor, working for candidates of various sizes, shapes, and ideologies. They had only two things in common.

First, all were Democrats.

Second, they were either ahead of their time, or behind it.

All I could be certain of, judging from the returns, was that they weren't on schedule.

Still, my own schedule for moving into the political PR big leagues proceeded. The big break came in May, 1958, when *Life* magazine shipped a correspondent and photographer down to cover the Alabama governor's race, one of those old-fashioned circus-style Deep South Democratic primaries. This one had fifteen candidates, including a midget and a piano player, and twelve assorted country music groups hired to work up crowds.

The leaders of the pack that spring were George Wallace, running his first state-wide race, and the man who finally won, John Patterson, who ran on a law-and-order ticket. Law and order in Alabama at that time meant defiance of the U.S. Supreme Court decision in the Brown case. This was the year Wallace lost because, as he was later quoted, he was "outsegged."

The candidate I handled, George Hawkins, speaker pro tem of the Alabama House, was a hard-nosed Methodist Sunday school-type who thought that law and order meant *abiding* by the *Brown* decision. This, in Alabama, in 1958! To make matters worse, Hawkins wouldn't even hire a country music group. He wasn't a born loser, just a principled one.

Hawkins called me up one afternoon in early spring to retain my PR services. He told me what he stood for and how he intended to campaign.

"You've got your PR man," I told him. "Now here's my first piece of professional advice. Withdraw."

"I'm running," he said.

"You'll lose," I said.

Which he did, and he did, running sixth in the field, but ahead of the midget and the piano player. Or as I euphemistically put it to him, in the upper quartile of his gubernatorial class.

But though Hawkins was a nonmusical ultra, I was sucessful, by means of various shticks, in getting him a full-page *Life* spread. George Wallace, Minnie Pearl, and other members of that year's political road show shared cramped quarters on the inside pages of the magazine.

It was a minor coup, another PR winner buried in a ballot-box disaster. This time, however, I left my candidate on better terms. Not only did Hawkins let me write his concession statement, he gave me his blessing seven months later when I packed in what was left of a law practice and headed for the Nation's Capital. Under my arm I carried a framed print of the *Life* spread with the inscription," To the best PR man in Alabama."

I hung it in my new office in Washington. But in all candor, I knew that somewhere, anesthetized by Kentucky's finest, Big Jim Folsom was still shaking his head.

What *is* public relations? Like the clients that PR men service, it's a business with an image far different from its substance.

In the beginning, when the business was young, PR men called themselves "propagandists" (after Pope Gregory XV's Congregation for the Propagation of the Faith). One of the founders of the profession, Edward Bernays, even wrote a book entitled *Propaganda*.

But that was before the First World War gave propaganda a bad name. So "propagandists" became "press agents." Then, in time, "press agentry" got a bad name. Leading to the euphemism, "public relations," and variations thereof: "public information," "public affairs," etc.

But whatever it's called, the game's the same—whether the client happens to be the President of the United States, Frank Sinatra, or Commercial Solvents, Inc.

"What's the Plant Food Institute?" I asked Sam Bledsoe, my first PR boss, not long after I arrived in Washington.

"An agri-business association," he replied. "Fertilizer interests."

"A lobby for bullshit?"

"I guess they *could* call it the Bullshit Institute," Sam shrugged, "but how would that distinguish it from any other lobby in town?"

Working the Commercial Solvents account in the early 1960s—that was the New York-based chemical firm represented by wheeler-dealer Billie Sol Estes while he was conning the farmers of Texas—I learned that in the euphemizing world of bigtime PR, bullshit isn't bullshit. At $3,000 a month, it's plant food. And when the fee climbs to $5,000—well, then it becomes something called anhydrous ammonia.

Commercial Solvents had its headquarters in Manhattan. Billie Sol Estes was the young Texas millionaire who had sold nonexistent anhydrous ammonia tanks to Texas farmers. Both the company and its agent had what Jeb Magruder would call "a little PR problem." Estes' problem went the way of Magruder's; he ended up serving time. Our job as a PR agency was to separate Commercial Solvents' corporate image from that of its convicted Texas sales rep.

Forty years ago, that kind of corporate PR problem would have been handled out of Manhattan, then the communications capital of the world. Those were the days when Business-was-Business and Government-was-Government. The centers of PR action were New York, Chicago, and Los Angeles.

But beginning in the 1950s, that center began to shift. A coaxial cable was stretched across the continent, bringing government and politics into the American living room via television. A decade later, John Kennedy, our first modern mediagenic President, changed the image of the Nation's Capital from that of a sleepy Southern town to a mecca of power and glamour. Washington, D.C., became the place to play the power game—the news capital where international and national images could be made or broken.

I was there when it happened. When the big industrial and commercial clients began hiring PR agencies not so much to push products and images on Madison Avenue, as to generate, or *un*-generate, action along Pennsylvania Avenue. When the men of political power started hiring

13

"media consultants" to deal with the new technology of mass communications. And when all the young, hungry anhydrous ammonia-slingers descended on the city, lured by the phantom of the image-making business.

What do they see that attracts them? What their fathers and older brothers saw when they descended on Hollywood West and Manhattan in former years. The lure in one form or another is power. The power that comes with fame, fortune, and political influence.

Mention "public relations" today and it conjures up the image of the power behind the throne, the fondler of brass rings for Presidents, Senators, Governors, and the great and rich of industry. Gray flannel eminences who plant words in the mouths of the mighty, manipulate the media, and who can make the worse appear the better cause.

So goes the image. Yet, look again at our public relations practitioner. Watch him closely, even as he entertains a columnist, client, or celebrity at "21" or Sans Souci. Note the furtive glance, the too-ready smile, all the telltale signs of a man leading a life of vociferous desperation.

Something is missing. True, he dresses well, picks up all the checks, belongs to the right clubs, and drops the right names. But is he the king's manipulator or just the king's eunuch? A power—or just a man close to power and the concubines, fated, by the limitations of his assignment, never to enjoy either?

What follows is one ring-polisher's answer to those questions. A personal view of the image and substance of power, politics, and public relations, recounted by a PR practitioner who abandoned his first passion for other pursuits.

Not an exposé. God knows, if there's anything this

country doesn't need until 1984, it's another Washington exposé. Or, if you're looking for a definitive work on the subject of public relations, this isn't that either. At least, not one likely to get the Public Relations Society of America's Good Euphemizing Seal of Approval.

Call it an apologia for misadventure that came about because one gray day in October, 1972, Arthur Sohmer, then Spiro Agnew's top administrative assistant, made a *pro forma* remark for that time and place.

I was in Sohmer's office, next to the then Vice President's, arguing that Agnew should or shouldn't do something—something that I knew, regardless of anything I said, he would or would not do anyway. The issue escapes me. It could have been a subject of vital importance, or maybe it was just something that had to do with the Presidential campaign against George McGovern. In any case, I was blowing hot and heavy when, suddenly, I heard Sohmer telling me . . .

"Of course," he was saying, "we all know that Spiro Agnew is Spiro Agnew's own best public relations man, so why argue?"

I stopped in mid-tantrum. *Where*, I asked myself, *have I heard a line like that before?*

It was the truth, of course. If Vic Gold were a better PR man than Spiro Agnew, then I'd be Vice President and he wouldn't, right?

Almost fourteen years to the day after I left Alabama —as PR time is measured, three dozen commercial and two dozen political clients—I'd come full circle on the merry-go-round. With or without the brass ring, it was time to get off.

My problem with Folsom had been that he didn't think I could do anything he couldn't do better for himself. It was the same problem with every client I'd worked for, commercial or political. Sooner or later, they don't need you when they're right *or* wrong. Anything you can do they can do better.

What's more, sitting there in Sohmer's office reflecting on a misspent middle age, I knew that my experience wasn't unique. Every PR man has the same problem. Public relations, you see, is simultaneously the world's most overrated and underrated way to earn a living.

Overrated because, in theory, there is that mystique of the image-maker, the manipulator of the art of modern power, with his mumbo-jumbo about demographics, samplings, motivational research, planned spontaneity, and media hypes.

Underrated because, in practice, for every PR professional in the field, there are tens of millions of lay experts —from your nearest Manhattan cab stand to 1600 Pennsylvania Avenue—each and every one of whom considers himself the world's foremost PR expert.

Am I communicating? If not, let me explain. Beginning, because of the way PR men are conditioned to think things through, at the end of the misadventure—Election Night, November 7, 1972. . . .

2. Night of Tri
u
m
p
h: I

It is wonderful to have a winner in politics . . .

Vice President Spiro T. Agnew,
Election Night, November 7, 1972

———◆———

The media called it an Administration of PR men, but it wasn't. By actual Public Relations Society of America count, there were only two people in the Nixon-Agnew staff structure who could claim credentials in real life as honest-to-God PR professionals: Bill Safire, the White House speechwriter, and myself.

True, there were ex-journalists with varying degrees of PR savvy. Herb Klein, Jim Keogh, Ray Price, and Pat Buchanan. And somewhere underneath that table of White House organization there was an operative named Howard Hunt who, among several other cover stories, passed as a PR man.

But mostly there were the technocrats, men with wild inner eyes like the Teutonic Knights, H. R. Haldeman and John Ehrlichman. Some were lawyers, with a penchant for ham-handed propaganda, others *merchandising*

17

men—there's a difference—whose PR sensibilities began and ended with decisions on the style and texture of the package.

The difference is that for all his argot about imagery, an authentic PR type occasionally expresses interest in the *product*. In his more public-spirited moments, he's even been known to ask not simply the *how* of a project, but the *why*.

By contrast, Nixon's White House experts on merchandise wrapping were men who spent hours, sometimes days developing such bright-ribboned refinements as:

> *When the Vice President stands alongside the President on the speaker's rostrum at the convention, make sure he doesn't raise his arms above his head. The President will wave to the convention delegates with arms extended only shoulder high.*

In two and a half years as Spiro Agnew's press secretary, I never failed to be baffled by such image-making subtleties, generally delivered as stage directions by *sotto voce* memorandum.

My professional PR experience shed no light on the subject. For that matter, I couldn't find any answers in available Library of Congress literature, e.g., *The New Style in Election Campaigns*, or anything Joseph Goebbels ever wrote about the psychology of mass rallies.

But most frustrating of all, the messenger for the chief merchandiser, when asked the simple question, "*Why?*" or "*Why not?*", would only shrug or wink unknowingly. Nixon White House code: *Never let your right hand know what your right hand is doing.*

O.K., orders are orders: remember, Spiro, arms only shoulder high. "*Why*," you ask? Because, if by some quirk of obstinacy or forgetfulness you and Nixon shoot your cuffs skyward on prime-time television, the ticket could end up losing two million votes. Five million, maybe. New York. Alaska. Not to mention Peoria.

Grown men took such matters seriously until they worked in the White House-Executive Office Building complex long enough to learn that these little packaging niceties weren't necessarily etched in granite.

Exhibit: What was the first thing Richard Nixon did after walking up the ramp to the speaker's rostrum at the Republican convention in 1972? He blew the whole White House script, two to five million votes—New York, Alaska, and Peoria—by grabbing his running mate's arm and lifting it, in the traditional gesture of campaigners, toward the convention hall ceiling.

Now, a little more than two months later, there was another scenario, this one hand-delivered from the White House west wing to key members of the Vice President's staff:

PRESIDENT'S ELECTION NIGHT APPEARANCE
Tuesday, November 7, 1972

BACKGROUND
The first appearance by either you or the Vice President will take place when it has been determined that you have been re-elected. . . .

SEQUENCE OF EVENTS

11:00 P.M. *(approx. 5 min.)*	You address the American people over live television from the Oval Office, which will be configured in the standard manner for television.
11:15 P.M. *(approx.)*	You and the First Family board motorcade on the South Driveway and depart en route Shoreham Hotel.

	Mrs. Nixon will ride with you, and Tricia and Ed and Julie and David will ride in a separate family car.
11:15 P.M. *(approx. 5 min.)*	The Vice President, accompanied by his family, will make his appearance at the Shoreham. The Vice President will declare victory for the Nixon-Agnew ticket, thank the campaign workers, and conclude his remarks by indicating that the President and the First Family are expected shortly.
11:20 P.M. *(approx.)*	The Vice President concludes and moves to stage left of the platform to await your appearance.

But wait: suppose the Vice President were to move stage *right*. Or even worse, run over his allotted speaking time?

Haldeman forbid! Once when Nixon returned from his trip to Peking, the Vice President's welcoming speech at Andrews Air Force Base ran eight minutes. While Agnew was on the platform extolling the success of the President's mission, Haldeman paced and fumed on the fringes of the welcoming crowd. Finally, when the speech reached six minutes, Haldeman confronted Pete Malatesta, one of Agnew's aides.

"Who wrote that goddamned speech?" he demanded, his face contorted in a spasm of autocratic apoplexy. *"We told you people it was to run only four minutes!"*

11:25 P.M. *(approx.)*	Your motorcade arrives at the entrance to the Shoreham Hotel.
	LIVE TELEVISION OF ARRIVAL

20

11:30 P.M. *(approx.)*	You and Mrs. Nixon and the First Family pause at the entrance for Ruffles and Flourishes and the following announcement:
	"Ladies and gentlemen, the President of the United States, Mrs. Nixon, and the First Family."
	LIVE TELEVISION OF ALL ACTIVITIES INSIDE BALLROOM
	The six of you enter to "Hail to the Chief" and move to the platform where the Vice President and family will be standing.
11:31 P.M. *(approx.)*	Your family will hold at stage right-rear of the platform as you go forward and take your applause.

So this was a landslide viewed from the mountaintop. Eight years before, I had witnessed it from the valley—without scenario—as Barry Goldwater's assistant press secretary.

Because I'd been with Goldwater, I could appreciate how the McGovernites felt, huddled around their television sets in a hotel headquarters somewhere in South Dakota, not far from Little Big Horn. Appreciate, mind you, not empathize or sympathize. To the true believer, political campaigning is the original form of cold war.

Once, in an early campaign, a candidate for whom I'd sweated blood and bile thought it would be magnanimous to walk down the street and personally congratulate his victorious opponent. I was outraged, until I realized, as my candidate smiled for the cameras, that this was the opening ploy in his next campaign.

To his credit, Goldwater took it grudgingly in '64. Not

21

in bad form, just grudgingly. There's a way to lose an election grudgingly, but in good form (Muskie could have taken lessons in the 1972 primaries). Goldwater knew how to pull it off. We were buried three minutes after the polls closed in New England, but Barry wouldn't concede until the next morning. The traveling press, especially the A.M. correspondents, screamed. The Democrats bitched about poor sportsmanship. Still, Goldwater had it figured right—extremely right.

Maybe he was simplistic, apolitical, out of sync with the *Zeitgeist*. But this much he knew: if you're a candidate running on ideology, you don't put twenty-seven million people on a crusade to save Western civilization from the depredations of Lyndon Johnson's Great Society, then cut it off like a faucet just because the depredators happen to *win*. The professionals can take defeat, but not the true believers. They have to be let down slowly. Lee didn't join Grant for cocktails and dinner. Magnanimity is a luxury for winners.

If you have to lose an election, though, landslides are the way to go. They do you in quick, early in the evening. Like biting into a cyanide pellet. The worst way is an upset, of course, and next to that, a squeaker that leaves you with the nagging question of whether one more (or less) appearance, one more (or less) television spot, one more nail for one more horseshoe, might have won the battle.

11:17 P.M. *"One of the things that satisfies me most about this election,"* Agnew was saying, on schedule and according to script, *"is the chance that I have had to be associated with a great President, a President whose policies have been put before the American people; a President who, the better he is known by the American people, the more he is loved by the American people."*

22

11:29 P.M. The Vice President concluded and moved, with Mrs. Agnew and family, stage left. Rising, sustained applause. Ruffles and Flourishes, "Hail to the Chief," then the President of the United States was speaking.

The speaker on the platform had experienced it all: the upset victory and the upset defeat, the squeaker won and the squeaker lost. Now, this night, the patron saint of working politicians was making restitution for all those hard times past. This victory celebration, scripted to the last detail, was the ultimate vindication of Richard Milhous Nixon.

I joined Spiro Agnew's staff as press secretary two years before, on another, less exhilarating election night. The question Washington image-watchers were asking the night of November 3, 1970—and would keep asking for twenty months—was what scenario Richard Nixon and his White House guard were working on for the 1972 Republican Vice Presidential nomination.

In the fall of 1970, they sent Agnew out on what amounted to a political anti-public relations mission, scripted down to the last controversial syllable of the last inflammatory word of the last abrasive speech. He was the Campaign '70 hatchetman, chopping away at Democratic Senate and House candidates in a six-week cross-country tour.

Bryce Harlow and Herb Klein, two White House staff members outside the Haldeman-Ehrlichman circle, brought me into the campaign to help with the care and feeding of the traveling press, as Agnew winged about the country delivering prepackaged attacks on "radiclibs" and "nattering nabobs of negativism."

My credentials for the assignment, incredibly, went back to the Goldwater disaster of '64. Goldwater had a

23

terrible press, but his press *relations* had been excellent.

Paul Wagner, Goldwater's campaign press secretary, and I had maintained credibility with members of the national media by providing straight answers and, among other comforts of home, sufficient laundry facilities along the campaign trail.

A national candidate's press relations can rise or fall on just such logistical detail. Hostile reporters describing a campaign appearance in two-day-old underwear will be twice as hostile as those seated by typewriters in freshly laundered shorts. (The problem escalates with *Ms.* reporters.)

Of course, there's a case to be made that the hostility quotient in Goldwater's campaign couldn't have been much worse if the traveling press had been sealed in six-day jocks. But the truth is that with few exceptions the reporters accompanying Goldwater weren't instinctively hostile to the candidate. They were gunning for Goldwater's conservative brand of Republicanism, not the man.

Add to that the fact that Goldwater wasn't so much a candidate as a Candide in his dealings with the smart-ass national press. He was a man with a penchant for the direct phrase when a euphemism might have served a better political purpose.

When Barry the Presidential candidate spoke without forked or mushed tongue, the traveling press made him an object lesson in why public figures with national ambitions shouldn't let it all hang out. The news business-as-practiced doesn't allow for fine distinctions. Qualifying phrases don't fit into headlines or three-minute network news reports.

The PR-minded politician keeps that in mind whenever someone shoves a notebook or microphone under his nose. He understands that on a slow news day reporters ask what Franklin Roosevelt once called "iffy" questions.

The fact that Goldwater wasn't PR-minded was his greatest strength as a candidate for *nomination*. He would answer "iffy" questions. It was also his greatest weakness as a candidate for *election,* because most answers to such questions are reported without the qualifying "if."

Exhibit: In Southern California my first day on the job during the 1964 campaign, a group of reporters cornered Goldwater aboard a yacht, the *Sundance,* in what was supposed to be an informal social interview preceding the official campaign kick-off. Within minutes, Bob Pierpoint of CBS was asking him an "iffy" question about the informal social matter of U.S. relations with what, in pre-Kissinger years, was called Red China.

The candidate's answer was lost to most staff members and press, because it came in an audio welter of Catalina Bay motorboat backfire. Not exactly a time or place to deliver a foreign policy pronouncement. But a question had been asked by a newsman and Goldwater wasn't one to duck. He replied—to the best of everyone's hearing—that given certain circumstances, he could foresee the possibility that one day the U.S. might have some form of relations with Mao's government.

An iffy answer to an iffy question. But the report went out from Catalina that if elected President, Goldwater might recognize Red China. Not exactly what the candidate said. Still, not exactly what he didn't say, either. So we had to issue a clarification putting the "if" back in. Then a second story ran, headlined GOLDWATER CLARIFIES RED CHINA STAND.

After a while, as a matter of policy, we stopped clarifying. We also stopped holding frequent news conferences. Given the Senator's refusal to duck questions and the traveling press' professional instinct for the neatly packaged news lead, we could have ended up Sundancing-and-clarifying into November.

Harlow and Klein considered my Goldwater experience the perfect requisite for helping Carl DeBloom, temporary press secretary, deal with the Agnew traveling press. The reason was that by 1970 Agnew had surpassed even Goldwater as the ideological bête noire of what Republicans, in the pre-Watergate era of unalloyed rancor, called the "Eastern Liberal Press."

Nothing the Arizona Senator said—including his geographically innovative recommendation that we saw off the Eastern seaboard and let it float into the Atlantic—bent the media's ideological antennae out of joint as much as the speeches Agnew delivered in Des Moines, Iowa, and Montgomery, Alabama, during the second and third weeks of 1969.

Those speeches—criticizing network news, *The New York Times,* and *The Washington Post*—instantly media-morphosed the Agnew image from Spiro the Boob to Spiro the Ogre. They also worked a profound change on the way Americans began to regard the Vice Presidency.

That was one of the attractions that led me to take a six-week leave from Victor Gold Associates for the fall, 1970, Agnew campaign.

It didn't take much time aboard the *Michelle Ann II,* Agnew's campaign aircraft named after his granddaughter, to recognize striking similarities between my new client's atypical approach to press relations and Barry Goldwater's.

Most political campaigners hound their press aides for bigger and better copy. On the Agnew tour, hunting conditions were reversed. It was the press that hounded, with the press aides at bay. The traveling bird dogs wanted interviews and copy that went deeper than speech handouts.

But Agnew had been burned by coverage during the 1968 Presidential campaign, and two years in the Vice President's office hadn't softened his attitude toward the press. In fact, it had hardened to a molecular density varying between quartz—after reading *The Washington Post* and *The New York Times*—and granite, later in the day, after reading Mary McGrory in the Washington *Evening Star-News.*

Long before I arrived on the job, Agnew had developed a foolproof defense against repeating his 1968 experience: an eleven-foot pole in his dealings with newsmen. For a PR man, this meant putting every professional instinct into reverse gear. Even when Agnew walked to the press section of his plane there wasn't any of the usual bonhomie between a campaigner and correspondents, because he wouldn't forget that his worst publicity during the 1968 campaign—the "fat Jap" episode—began with a casual remark to traveling newsmen.

Agnew and Goldwater shared another atypical political trait running counter to PR instinct. DeGaulle-like, they both shunned standard political publicity gimmicks.

My memory of Barry Goldwater's most pained moment during the 1964 campaign isn't the candidate conceding a landslide defeat. It was when he posed in an engineer's cap at the throttle of a campaign train during a whistle-stop tour.

"Senator, would you mind sliding over to the next throttle?" I asked. "The photographers want to shoot from your left side."

"To hell with it," Goldwater snapped, his face flushed beneath the unwanted cap. "I'm here now, and it's as far as I'll go."

Agnew also had an aversion to photo gimmicks, but he differed from Goldwater in his appreciation for the graphic phrase. This was the penchant for verbal fireworks the Nixon White House exploited during Campaign '70. It was the season of acidulous alliteration. But when the fun and word games were over, no one was more aware that Spiro Agnew had been used than Spiro Agnew himself. All he had to show for his effort was a plummeting Gallup rating and the White House Good Conduct Medal for political kamikaze.

Contrary to what was said during the Nixon-Agnew years, this wasn't the way Presidents have used their Vice Presidents through history. Most of the time, they haven't used them at all. But after the 1948 election, Harry Truman had a special problem with his Vice President, Alben Barkley (the first to be called "Veep"). Barkley had been Senate Majority Leader. Truman felt he couldn't neglect his No. 2 man, who was a Democratic elder statesman. So "Dear Alben" was put out on the road as a party fundraiser.

In the early 1950s, during my Young Democrat days, I handled press relations for a party banquet featuring Barkley as the main speaker. He was the best political storyteller in the business back then, one of a dying breed of orators whose last surviving member is probably Senator Sam Ervin.

As I recall, the Veep laid it into Republicans pretty well that night. But in an old-fashioned spellbinder's way. The Vice President as Political Hatchetman had not become an institution. That didn't occur until Nixon was put on the road during the Eisenhower years.

Nixon tried to pattern his White House image along Eisenhower's lines: the President above politics. The image fit, as Earl Long used to say, like socks on a rooster. But that was what the Nixonites called the Big Game Plan, and Agnew's assignment was to play Nixon's old position.

Agnew, of course, didn't *have* to play the game. Nothing in the U.S. Constitution says that a Vice President has to serve as lackey to a White House master. But No. 2 men in recent times have gone along with Presidents because of their own game plans for the future.

Like Hubert Humphrey before him, Agnew was awed by the Oval Office and its inhabitant. Nixon didn't snap orders like Lyndon Johnson, but Agnew felt that if he was ever going to get into the Oval Office himself, he had to have Nixon's support. And so, just as HHH jumped through hoops for LBJ because of his ambition to succeed to the Presidency, STA, for all his tough exterior, was a cream puff when it came to bucking White House directives. Except one time, when he drew the line at going to a Gridiron Club dinner. More on that later.

Back now to Election Night, 1970. The Vice President had invited Cabinet members and families to join him and Judy Agnew in watching returns at the Washington Hilton. It was a memorable evening for me because of two incidents—one of World Historical importance, the other personal.

The World Historical incident involved Attorney General John Mitchell and his flaky wife. The rise and fall of Martha Mitchell during the Nixon years epitomizes Washington's new status as Hollywood East, where the alchemy of power and celebrity can work wonders in transmuting images.

Martha Mitchell was simply one of many Cabinet wives until she established herself as an addle-tongued interview subject. Her exposure on national television, sounding off on issues of the day, was a continuing source of embarrassment to the Nixon White House—an unmanageable PR problem that grew worse with the passage of time.

By November, 1970, Martha had become a national personality, a self-made PR creation. Her popularity among Republican fund-raising dinner chairmen was at its height. The Washington press corps viewed her as an oasis of volatility in the desert of Nixonian social life.

The image the woman projected—a Tennessee Williams character in search of a Gore Vidal play—was doomed to self-destruct through overexposure. But that couldn't have mattered less to those in the media exploiting her idiosyncracies for their own fast-news-buck purposes.

Election Night, 1970, Martha was at Agnew's party, eyes sparkling, resplendent in a white dinner gown, the heroine of Middle American Republican straights who, if her husband hadn't been Attorney General, would have put her down as a hyperthyroid neighborhood nuisance.

Six telephones had been installed in the suite so the Vice President could call Republican candidates around the country, congratulating winners and expressing condolences to losers. However, as the evening wore on and Martha's spirits soared, it became clear that sooner or later there was going to be a problem with the phones.

It came, sooner *and* later. At nine o'clock, the idea occurred to Martha that *she* ought to call Republican candidates, too. By ten o'clock, she was moving between two phones. By midnight, she was ricocheting off all six, and Agnew was fuming.

Finally, in the early A.M., John Mitchell, who'd been puffing his pipe and letting the inevitable happen, indicated enough was enough. Big John rose from his chair.

"All right, that's it," he snapped. "Let's go."

It was a directive delivered in a tone that would have sent three hundred junior members of the largest law firms in New York City stampeding for the nearest door.

Unfortunately, Martha Mitchell had never worked as a junior law clerk, so the message didn't get through right away. In time, however—about two hours later—law and order prevailed. The Mitchells departed, arm in arm. White House signal operators went off Mayday frequency. And Spiro Agnew got a crack at his own telephones.

The second memorable incident of the evening occurred before Martha went onto her phone jag. Agnew asked me to take on the job as his press secretary. Carl DeBloom was heading back to Columbus, Ohio, after his leave of absence from the *Dispatch*. Having kept the traveling press in clean shorts during Campaign '70, I was recommended as a PR pro who might help the Vice President's long-range press relations.

Politicians can survive combat with the press and some actually benefit from it. But no man in public life really likes going to war with the people who report his activities. Hope breathes eternal—or at least until the next election—that somehow press relations can be improved. I think Agnew had that in mind when he hired me.

Or was it that? Maybe all he had in mind was somebody who could be a buffer state while the war went on. I'd been around long enough to know that people who retain PR men do it with mixed feelings. They hire the men, not the public relations.

Somebody once commented that all Spiro Agnew wanted from a press secretary was a voice on the line when a newsman called, a recording to say, "Screw you." Nothing more, or less. I hadn't heard that story when the Vice President offered me the press secretary's job, but it didn't take me long to discover that my new client expected very little in the way of unsolicited PR advice.

"Mr. Vice President," I counseled at 11:00 P.M., while

Agnew was trying to squeeze in a call on one of Martha's party lines, "if you want to catch the large Eastern audience, it's time to go to the network cameras."

"I'll get around to it," he nodded.

"You know, the Eastern audience starts tuning out . . ."

"Let *me* worry about the size of my audiences," he said.

Thirty minutes later, I tried again.

"Victor," he said, stone-faced and cool, "I said I'd get around to it, didn't I? And if I don't, well, I don't."

When he finally went to the cameras it was three-thirty in the morning. Not a total loss, I told my wife as we headed home. After all, the East Coast has a lot of insomniacs who don't watch late-night Ronald Reagan movies.

It was an omen. But aside from Billy Graham and Jeane Dixon, who in Washington was into omens in those days?

3. Who Was That Rhino I Saw You With Last Night?

The counsel on public relations is what sociologists call a societal technician who is fitted by training and experience to evaluate the maladjustments and adjustments between his client and the publics upon whom the client is dependent for his socially sound activity.

Edward Bernays, *Theory of Public Relations*

Throw your dart against the wall, then draw a circle around it. That was the target.

Ben Sonnenberg, *Theory of Public Relations*

———◆———

As a child of the power structure, public relations as a profession was unimmaculately conceived by not one, but *two* fathers. The first was Ivy Lee, who handled John D. Rockefeller, Jr., and Standard Oil. The second was Edward Bernays, whose early list of blue-chip clients included Thomas Masaryk, the George Washington of Czechoslovakia.

According to Bernays—the prototype of the PR man who isn't shy about publicizing his role in history—he advised Masaryk over a meal at Delmonico's in 1919 to declare Czech independence on a Sunday. Why? Because Sunday is supposed to be a slow news day.

This remains one of the truisms of the PR trade, despite the fact that Waterloo, Custer's Last Stand, the

Chicago Fire, the declaration of Czech independence, and Pearl Harbor all took place on Sundays.

In any event or Sunday scheduling thereof, an instinct for dates remains an important part of a professional PR man's repertoire. It may even pass for a sense of history.

Datesmanship has become a remunerative PR specialty in its own right. The Civil War Sesquicentennial was a PR/advertising bonanza. But it was only a huckster's warm-up for the national Bicentennial, which promises to eclipse all previous merchandising and image-making spin-offs.

On a less epochal level, exploiting dates figured into some of my own Great Moments in PR History. There was that memorable National Coffee Day on Capitol Hill in 1959, when I threw a Hawaiian coffee break in honor of the Pan-American Coffee Queen: pineapple juice mixed with coffee grown in America's 50th State. Very memorable.

On the other hand, not knowing that July 19 is the national holiday of Franco's Spain was a personal nadir in a four-week round-the-world Vice Presidential trip described by *Time* magazine in August, 1971, as a "public relations disaster."

But first, the Up dates. Before the Goldwater campaign, my greatest contribution to history was getting Sir Winston Churchill appointed a Kentucky colonel on the occasion of his first July Fourth as an honorary U.S. citizen.

Working as the Bourbon Institute account man in Washington, I was always on the alert for ways to impress superpatriotic elbow benders with the fact that bourbon—not Brand X distilled in those foreign highlands—is the native American whiskey. And so, when Congress passed a bill in April of 1963 declaring Churchill an honorary citizen, it occurred to me that Sir Winston ought to toast his first Independence Day as a 100 percent American with a 100 percent American drink. Coca-Cola wasn't what I had in mind.

The problem was that the only way to involve a World Historical Figure in a crass commercial hype is by way of a cover hype. A Kentucky colonelcy was the solution. Kentucky's Governor at the time, a genial Democrat named Bert Coombs, was happy to oblige. The case of Kentucky-made bourbon was shipped along, after appropriate photo-sessions for the wire services, as a token of the State's esteem.

History records Sir Winston as one of the world's great brandy drinkers, so whether he actually even saw the bourbon is questionable. But a few days after it was delivered, Bill Marshall, the Institute president, received a Churchillian cable direct from Ari Onassis' yacht: "I AM DEEPLY OBLIGED TO THE STATE OF KENTUCKY FOR THE AGREEABLE COMPLIMENT WHICH YOU HAVE PAID ME . . ." The promotion received heavy holiday play across the country—WINNIE RECEIVES BOURBON, COLONELCY FROM KENTUCKY. Considering my disloyalty to bourbon in personal drinking habits, I look back on the Churchill caper as my finest hour in commercial public relations.

In a way, Churchill was also the historical catalyst for my most memorable dating experience during the Goldwater campaign of 1964.

As a speechwriter for hawkish Senators and Congressmen during the Viet Nam sixties, I was a heavy Churchill quoter, relying on what Arthur Schlesinger, Jr., and other doves were then denouncing as "the discredited Munich analogy." That is, the parallel drawn by hawks between

Communist aggression in the sixties and Nazi aggression in the thirties.

I hadn't been hired as a Goldwater speechwriter. But two hours before the Senator was scheduled to kick off his Presidential campaign in Prescott, Arizona, my eye fell on the dateline to an advance story being hacked out by Joe Sterne of the *Baltimore Sun*.

It was September 3. To a professional PR date buff, this trivia immediately registered as the twenty-fifth Anniversary of England's declaration of war against Nazi Germany. I advised Paul Wagner, the press secretary, of my discovery.

"It's also the thirty-fourth Anniversary of the Great San Domingo hurricane," Wagner shrugged. "What's your point?"

I quickly explained that a discredited Munich analogy seemed in order for the Senator's kick-off speech. Wagner nodded and said he would see whether Goldwater would consider a speech insert. Provided I wrote it up, on the spot. So I sat down on a dusty curb in Prescott, Arizona, and proceeded to write for posterity.

Raw meat for the right-wing masses. All about how a quarter-century before, *on this very day, at this very hour,* England had to enter a war unprepared because of timid, narrow-visioned leadership. And how Lyndon Johnson, a tool of the Council on Foreign Relations, was taking America down the same path.

I passed my prime-rib prose along to Wagner in scribbled longhand. He headed in the general direction of Denny Kitchell, Goldwater's campaign manager. Ten minutes before the Senator was introduced on the platform, Wagner approached me as I stood alongside the press area. He had good news. Or did he?

"Congratulations," he said. "Goldie's using part of

your insert." Then Wagner pulled on his cigar stub and scanned the shirt-sleeved crowd spread from the Prescott courthouse steps to the street beyond. "You're *sure* about that date?"

"Hell yes, I'm sure," I said.

"Good," he nodded, "because if you're wrong, the next plane doesn't leave Prescott for three days. You're fired." He was serious.

"You'd fire me?" I asked, "for one pissant reference in a speech?"

"If you don't know it by now, let me tell you," Wagner said, a fraternal hand on my shoulder. "In Presidential politics, there are no pissant references."

He was right, of course. As the incident on the *Sundance* proved, Goldwater had no margin for error. The most innocuous fluff would be headlined as another example of the candidate's political boobery. Eight years later, George McGovern's press aide, Dick Daugherty, complained about the same press penchant for developing candidate stereotypes early in a campaign, then zeroing in on the slightest trivia to support their thesis.

Now Wagner was satisfied about the date. But suddenly *I* wasn't. Suppose my datesman's instinct had failed me this one time?

GOLDWATER GOOFS AGAIN
Misdates Start of Second World War
in Arizona Kick-Off Speech

Sweating under a hot sun, I could see the black headline looming above the Arizona hills in the distance. The headline and all that could follow. An Art Buchwald column. A Herblock cartoon. A *New Yorker* zap. A protest letter from the American Association for the Preservation of the Memory of the Origin of the Second World

War (there was bound to be one). An Evans-Novak column needling us for sloppy staff work . . .

> The appalling disarray of the Goldwater Presidential campaign was never more apparent, according to well-informed Republican insiders, than when the candidate, only five minutes into his opening speech, made a glaringly inaccurate reference to the beginning of the Second World War . . .

Not to mention what Arthur Schlesinger, Jr., writing in *The London Times,* would have to say about spurious discredited analogies.

All a bad mirage. Wagner and I were just being paranoid. But the staff of a politician repeatedly hit by levitating verbal furniture tends to see and hear editorial poltergeists. This is especially true of professionals hired to keep a political principal *out* of trouble with the press. For the PR man, the ultimate offense is to offer counsel that leads to a gaffe. Such as an incorrect date. Or an inaccurate pronunciation.

Take the name Jomo Kenyatta. Is it pronounced *Jomo* or *Yomo?*

Spiro Agnew asked that question one afternoon in July, 1071. We were in his hotel suite in downtown Nairobi, guarded outside by two dozen U.S. Secret Service men and a dozen of Jomo Kenyatta's special Mau-Mau police, a standard entourage for visiting dignitaries, I was told. But still, disquieting.

At least, I was disquieted. I took one look at the Mau-Maus in the hotel corridor and bolted straight for Sam Sulliman and John Simpson, who headed Agnew security.

"Can you handle those bastards if they revert to type in the middle of the night?" I asked Sulliman.

"Let's make a deal," he said. "We worry about the Mau-Mau guards and you worry about the Mau-Mau press."

Fair enough. So while the Vice President relaxed on a couch and reviewed the remarks he planned to make before a native Kenyan audience that evening, I looked out a window toward the city of Nairobi and cogitated a nagging PR problem involving the local *Newsweek* stringer.

"Is it *Jomo* or *Yomo?*" Agnew suddenly asked.

"Huh?"

"Is it *Jomo* or *Yomo?*" he said.

Now, it probably comes as a shock to most people that any man one heartbeat away from running American foreign policy would have to ask his press secretary that kind of trivia. There's this myth, you see, that once a man reaches a certain level of power, he automatically either knows or is geared to a failsafe system that informs him about such matters. A system, that is, other than asking a press secretary.

This view is comforting, but naive. Like any large organization, the U.S. Government suffers from cracks through which small, piddling details escape. So it was that a President, John Kennedy, could appear on national television to talk about a possible U.S.-Communist confrontation in a country he called—until later corrected—"Lay-oss." And a Vice President, though briefed on all the major outstanding problems between the U.S. and a country he was visiting, could wonder about a fairly significant native pronounciation.

Somewhere someone had blundered. The phonetic breakdown on Jomo Kenyatta's name hadn't been included in Agnew's State Department briefing book. So he turned to me, which was perfectly logical under the circumstances. First, I was the PR man paid to plug up cracks. Second, I was the Agnew staff's leading trivia expert.

"Who was that San Diego back that did so well—when was it—two, three weeks ago, on the Monday night game?" Agnew would call to ask.

"Cid Edwards," I'd reply, no hesitation. "Spelled *C-i-d*, not *S-i-d*."

"Yeah, that's right." Then he'd hang up.

Now, a man who knows that Cid Edwards spells it with a "*C*" not an "*S*" can be counted on when a failsafe system fails. So Agnew turned to me that afternoon in Nairobi. And I, who should have had sense enough to refer the question to Mike Dunn, his foreign policy aide, came through.

"Yomo," I replied.

"You're sure?" Agnew asked.

I nodded, yes.

What I needed right then, of course, was Paul Wagner to give me the timetable on the next plane from Nairobi to Washington. Unlike the situation in Prescott, there was time to check. But I didn't. Instead, that minor interruption over, I turned back to the problem of *Newsweek*'s African correspondent.

Andrew Jaffe (pronounced *Jaffe,* not *Yaffe*) was a Mau-Mau journalist waiting in the bush to savage a visiting American Vice President. He wasn't the first Mau-Mau I ever ran into, only the first to con me. I came away from Kenya more convinced than ever that what some people call the New Journalism requires a New Press Relations to cope with it.

I don't know who should be called the Father of Mau-Mau Journalism, but I do know that the man they tried to pin it on denied paternity.

"There was a piece the other day written by Jack

Newfield," wrote Jimmy Cannon not long before he died. "It was a serious piece in which he said that the New Journalism that all these guys are now claiming as their own was started by me thirty years ago. I'm perfectly willing to take the bow. But I've got to add something else—the so-called New Journalism was the iceberg that sank the *Herald Tribune.*

"And if the New Journalists are my bastard children, I want to disown them. I prefer them not to bear my name. My main objection to some of them is that they make up quotes. They invent actions. When I was a kid we used to call it faking and piping, smoking the pipe, opium smoking."

Iconoclast journalists who take on public gods are nothing new, of course. Jack Anderson is the foremost current exponent of a muckraking school whose mission is to make life miserable for officialdom. Bob Woodward and Carl Bernstein are members of a younger generation carrying on the same tradition.

As Agnew's press secretary, I got several calls a month from Anderson. He'd tell me he was onto something about Agnew. Would I care to add to it, deny it, or explain Agnew's side of the story?

But the fundamental difference between a genuine investigative reporter like Anderson and a Mau-Mau journalist like, say, Joe McGinniss, is that Anderson doesn't smoke the pipe in putting his stories together. Nor is there any deception involved in the way the Andersons and Woodward-Bernsteins gain access to their information. They come at a story as reporters-in-reporters' clothing, not under camouflage.

I made it a practice never to answer a phone call from McGinniss because he has a gift for piping even a "No comment" into six paragraphs of bright prose. Here, after all, was a reporter who made his first big national score by conning the Nixon staff during the 1968 Presidential campaign.

That was the year McGinniss told Harry Treleavan, the Nixon PR pro, that he was a graduate student doing a research paper on political campaigning. Treleavan gave McGinniss access to the candidate and inner workings of the campaign. Result: *The Selling of the President, 1968,* a book based on confidential material the reporter squirreled away during his travels with the Nixon inner circle.

With publication of *The Selling of the President, 1968,* liberal Democrats howled with glee. McGinniss was an instant New Journalist folk hero. Then, four years later, the same reporter conned George McGovern into a buddy-buddy conversation about the 1972 Presidential race. Result: a head-chopping magazine piece, complete with "honest" Mau-Mau coverage of Eleanor McGovern's reaction to campaign stress.

The trouble with the Mau-Maus is that they follow no guidelines in covering a story except their own egos. McGinniss and his type are to political reportage what Chuck Colson was to the Nixon White House: they'd walk over their own grandmothers to turn in smart-ass copy.

Even before Treleavan was burned in 1968, however, I was wary of giving potential Mau-Maus access to a candidate during a campaign. My own guideline was that an accredited journalist—this includes Joe McGinniss and even the *Village Voice* correspondent—has an absolute right to cover all public functions where the candidate appears. But personal access—for that matter, being a member of the candidate's personal press entourage—is something else again. They're entitled to a seat in the press section of the auditorium. On the other hand, having their hotel reservations made and laundry arranged by a candidate's press aide isn't a First Amendment right—despite anything Jack Newfield's *Voice* may have to say on the subject.

The *Voice* faulted me for this policy during the 1972 campaign after I wouldn't make arrangements to carry one of their correspondents on an Agnew campaign trip. My decision was based on what the *Voice*'s correspondent did—or claimed he did—on the Agnew plane in 1968.

That campaign year the *Voice* featured a front-page "campaign" story detailing their correspondent's exploits on a swing through the Southwest as part of the Agnew traveling press. The story told of the correspondent's crossing the border to Mexico on one stopover, buying a load of Acapulco Gold, and carrying the contraband back to Washington on the Agnew plane.

The thrust of the piece was that law-and-order Agnew and his staff, shmucks that they were, helped transport pot into the country without knowing it. I read the story and filed it. When the *Voice* had the chutzpah to demand a place on board the '72 plane, I referred their correspondent to that 1968 story. He was outraged. Called me "uptight." Uptight, maybe, but a shmuck, no.

A New Public Relations to cope with a New Journalism. But still, even the most uptight New PR Man can slip up. After all, every traditional PR instinct is directed toward opening doors to the press. You want your client to give reporters access. While understanding the risks and adversary nature of the politician-journalist relationship, the PR man takes the position that it's best to deal with a Jack Anderson directly. Get your side of the story out. Trust to a reporter's fairness and the public's good judgment.

Encountering one Joe McGinniss or Andrew Jaffe

changes all that. The trauma of being had by an in-gratiating newsperson with a machete hidden beneath journalistic credentials can jaundice a PR man's future attitude toward strangers in the media.

The specific problem bugging me when Agnew asked the *Jomo* question was whether to give Jaffe a free trip to Treetops, the famous hunting lodge fifty miles from Nairobi. Since *Newsweek* hadn't assigned a full-time cor-respondent to our entourage, the issue was whether letting Jaffe join our entourage for a single excursion would be fair to *Time*, whose correspondent, Hays Gorey, was pay-ing full fare. Sleeping accommodations at Treetops were limited, so to include Jaffe would mean asking one of our full-trip correspondents to double up in a room.

Over a gin and tonic at the circular bar on the roof of the Nairobi Hilton, Jaffe appealed to my sense of fair play. True, he said, *Newsweek* hadn't seen fit to cover the full trip. But why should he, an American corres-pondent in Africa trying to cover his Vice President, have to suffer for the stupidity of New York editors? He wanted to cover Agnew's trip "fully and fairly," Jaffe said. The only way he could do that was by being on the scene when Agnew visited Kenya's best-known tourist attrac-tion.

"The Kenyans are impressed with Agnew," Jaffe told me, "they like his style. He's making a better impression than any American official who ever visited here before, including Bobby Kennedy."

Bullshit, of course. But I sat listening and decided to open the door. Not because I thought Jaffe was a journalistic hooker guaranteed to hype my client's image. I knew better than that. Working for Barry Goldwater and Spiro Agnew, I'd come to settle for a 50-50 break with national magazines. Which is all I hoped for when

Jaffe boarded the press bus and the Agnew motorcade moved out of Nairobi the following afternoon, en route to Treetops.

Treetops is an enlarged cabin on stilts overlooking a mud salt lick in a jungle clearing. A plaque on the outside veranda commemorates the fact that it was here Elizabeth II climbed the stairs a Princess one afternoon and descended a Queen the following morning.

There were thirty-five guests in the cabin resort that night, including the Kenyan Minister of Tourism, the Provincial Commissioner, the Director of National Parks, half a dozen wildlife experts, three U.S. Embassy officials, fifteen members of the press, and the Agnew traveling staff. Among the latter were his secretary, Mary Ellen Warner, and his official physician from the Navy Department, William Voss.

After a dinner of venison and other native delicacies, the group gathered near the picture window running the length of the cabin. The Treetops routine is to gaze down on big game gathered around a mud salt lick. Never having been a wildlife buff, I watched for an hour before turning toward the cabin bar with the comment, reported back to the States by New York *Times* correspondent Bob Semple, that "If you've seen one elephant, you've seen 'em all."

Along about midnight, one of the Treetops guides pointed toward a distant clump at the far end of the mud lick.

"Look out theah," he said, in clipped British. "Tyoo rhinos cawpulating."

It was a switch, so I joined the group at the window. Up to that point it had been all elephant herds and water buffalo, sucking mud. As it turned out, copulating rhinoceri, viewed at 1,000 feet, offer about the same thrill. A

Last Tango in Kenya it wasn't. But it turned out to be exactly what Andrew Jaffe was looking and listening for to flesh out his full and fair coverage of Agnew's visit to Kenya.

I read the story sitting down—on the advice of friends in the traveling press entourage—after we left Africa. Sipping sangria at Soto Grande on the Costa del Sol.

"Aside from hacking up a local golf course," *Newsweek* reported—the high point of accuracy in a story headlined SAFARI—"[Agnew's] main outing was to a nearby hunting lodge, where in company with his private physician and pretty, red-haired secretary, he watched two rhinos copulating."

So what happened to the thirty-two other people? More to the point, I asked myself as a PR man, what would have happened if I'd told Jaffe we just weren't going to double-up traveling press in order to accommodate him? That his New York editors were *his* problem, not mine?

Poor PR, by the old rules. But there would have been no copulating rhinos story to stir a minor sensation back in Washington. Not one of the rest of the attendant press considered the incident worth reporting. And yes, there was that one other item that no one else—not even the Kenyan press—had noted.

It was the pissant reference. The detail left unchecked because I'd been engrossed in pondering the equity of taking Andrew Jaffe to Treetops. Among the other gaffes listed in *Newsweek*'s coverage of Agnew's Kenya trip was a one-line mention that he "referred to Jomo Kenyatta as Yomo Kenyatta."

I put down the magazine and ordered another sangria. Andrew Jaffe was then several thousand miles to the south. I fantasized him in the vanguard of a bevy of crocodiles, or, better still, a few of those real Mau-Maus that Jomo keeps around him. No such luck, I knew. But I was in luck of another kind. A short, swarthy stranger approached the table.

"Are you Vic Gold?" he asked.

"Yeah."

He held out his hand. "I'm Miguel Acoco, *Newsweek's* correspondent in these parts . . ."

Foreign travel is broadening, saith the political PR Bible. The politician with an eye on bigger things, like an applicant to the Civil Air Patrol, is expected to put in a requisite number of hours-in-flight.

The recipe for getting the most PR mileage out of overseas trips is standard.

First, get your picture taken with world leaders (King Faisal for the ambitious Texan, Moshe Dayan for the ambitious New Yorker).

Next, spend two or three days touring historic sites in the foreign capital, laying a few wreaths here and there (on camera, of course).

Then, follow that up with a day in the country, talking to colorful natives in order to get the real "feel" of the land (informal news conference with American and foreign press afterwards).

Voila! You're a foreign policy expert.

For a repeat performance two or three years later: throw in a side trip to a local flea or fish market; keep your PR man's eye peeled for a character, say a camel driver, for a sound-on-film invitation, with interpreter's help, to visit the United States.

Voila! You're an expert with oak leaf clusters for the "human touch."

Anyone can do it in the Jet Age, and as former mayor

of Los Angeles Sam Yorty proved, some can even *overdo* it. But the man who started it all, the pioneer of instant foreign expertise back in the rugged days of propeller travel, was Richard Nixon.

Just as Lyndon Johnson's rapport with a camel driver reflected his penchant for garish PR flourishes, Nixon's human touch clusters were unique to his style. He was stoned in Caracas and got involved in a head-to-head debate with Nikita Khrushchev on the relative merits of American and Soviet life. The former event was an unscheduled bit of political fortune. But the latter was one in which Bill Safire, then a New York PR man, played the part of historical catalyst.

Safire was in Moscow representing a company displaying a model American kitchen at the Moscow Trade Fair. Serving as host at the U.S. exhibit, Vice President Nixon escorted Premier Khrushchev to the U.S. exhibit area, heading directly for the model kitchen display. Only those who didn't know Safire considered that move accidentally fortuitous to the PR man's client. The "Kitchen Debate," as it came to be called, developed as a spontaneous bonus to both the client and Nixon's political aspirations.

From Caracas to Moscow and points in between, Nixon during the 1950s broke all previous records for overseas hours-in-flight by an American official other than a Secretary of State. Some of those records, like his seventy-day-plus round-the-world tour, still stand as public relations models for Vice Presidents in search of an image-building way to escape the trap of political nonentity that goes with the office.

Only a month before the moment in PR history when I told *Newsweek*'s Costa del Sol correspondent to go screw a rhinoceros, Spiro Agnew's thirty-one-day round-the-world trip had begun in Seoul, Korea, where he headed the official U.S. delegation to the inauguration of President Park Chung Hee. It was here that the seeds of public relations disaster were sown among a traveling press that spent six full days socked into a hotel lobby with no hard news.

Agnew had previous foreign travel experience. But his chief PR man didn't. I knew, however, that in handling official publicity overseas, my normal manic approach to domestic PR assignments would be out of order. Never did I instinctively size up a professional problem any better.

On those few occasions when I forgot where I was, results ranged from ineffective to perilous. Shouting at a Turkish driver to keep up with an official motorcade, for example, isn't the same as leaning on a busman in Peoria. In Ankara, a driver who doesn't understand plain, shouted English just shrugs and keeps moving ahead at his usual ten k.p.h.

In Kenya, on the other hand, a press busman who does understand—having been trained in the British military disciplines—pushes the accelerator through the floorboard, passes half a dozen dignitary cars, and has to be physically restrained from taking the press contingent over the side of a cliff.

Still, that kind of logistical problem is minor compared to more substantial dangers that await the unsuspecting American PR man on his first overseas mission.

Another of my decisions before we left the West Coast for Seoul, Korea, was that I would at all times be courteous but totally unresponsive to members of the foreign press in countries where there was a language difference. This was Ugly Americanism, but the better part of PR wisdom, as I learned our second day in Seoul.

Agnew and South Korean President Park were scheduled to meet at a luncheon. Yet, at 10:30 A.M., I picked up a copy of the leading Korean-English language daily and read a detailed summary of what *had been* discussed at the meeting. Complete with direct quotes.

Since the Agnew-Park luncheon story referred to substantive discussions concerning U.S. arms commitments to South Korea, it couldn't be ignored.

"What's this all about?" I asked Mort Smith, then head of the U.S. Information Agency office in South Korea. USIA is the country's PR arm overseas. Despite the scars it bears from two decades of political buffeting, Left and Right, the agency's offices are an indispensable link between visiting American officials and the foreign media.

Smith went to the phone to check out the matter. Twenty minutes later the USIA bureau chief reported back. He had been involved in one of those gracious, Oriental 'round-Robin Hood's-pagoda discussions with the Korean editor of the paper, who admitted that, yes, the story was "premature," i.e., simultaneous translation from euphemistic Korean, "concocted." But we had to understand *his* problem.

"You see," he explained, "we have an early deadline."

One week later, in Kuwait, I was shaken awake one broiling morning by Secret Service agent Tobey Chandler, who alerted me to an interview with the U.S. Ambassador on the front page of the local English-language paper. The Ambassador was directly quoted to the effect that the Vice President's visit to the country was part of a U.S. plot to advance the purposes of international Zionism.

I contacted the Ambassador. He told me (as I suspected) that the interview had never taken place. Pressed as to how he obtained his direct quotes, the Kuwaiti editor later carried the Seoul Principle of Prematurity one step ahead. He had "constructed" the conversation, he said, based on what he "felt" were the Ambassador's ideas on the subject.

After a news conference at which the Ambassador denied the interview, I told Agnew that he had to readjust our thinking about the media back home. Eastern Liberal élitism was nothing compared to the Far and Mid-Eastern variety. Two weeks on the overseas circuit had made me homesick for *The New York Times* and *The Washington Post*.

Meanwhile, back at 1600 Pennsylvania Avenue, even as Spiro Agnew prepared to leave the Middle East for Africa, some of the President's top PR aides were deep into a campaign to cut down the image of the Vice President as Foreign Policy Expert.

At the time, along with other members of the Vice President's staff, I thought this counter PR was the work of White House operatives acting on their own. Later it became obvious that Nixon himself was encouraging White House leaks downgrading his Vice President and upgrading the man he then wanted as his 1972 running mate, John Connally.

Another John—John Scali, slated to become U.S. Ambassador to the United Nations—was the sub-Rose Garden director of the anti-Agnew campaign in the foreign policy area. Scali had been named to the White House staff as an international PR consultant. A onetime AP and ABC correspondent, Scali had wide contacts among Washington and foreign newsmen. He was a master at the PR skill of P&L: Planting and Leaking stories.

The Agnew traveling party was in Zaire (formerly

the Belgian Congo) when the White House announced the secret Kissinger mission to Peking. Henry was being sent to arrange the President's forthcoming visit to the People's Republic of China (formerly Red China). After returning to the States, I learned Scali was the source of a White House leak to newsmen pointing out that the announcement had been made while the Vice President was in the African wilds. What's more, according to the Scali leak, Agnew hadn't been informed in advance of the President's planned China trip.

When members of our news-starved traveling press party were cabled about the leak by their Washington editors, they fell on the story like hounds on filet. Had the Vice President really been left in the dark about the China trip? I gave them a euphemistic reply.

Sure, I said, Agnew knew. He was a member of the National Security Council, wasn't he? That kept him "fully apprised" of all foreign policy developments. This statement was accurate as far as it went. But the traveling press correctly sensed that a PR man's answer which takes a circuitous route is evading some main point. Which was exactly what I was trying to do.

The White House had deliberately, not accidentally, screwed Agnew by withholding advance word on the timing of the China announcement. Agnew knew there was going to be a China trip, all right, for the reason I gave. As an NSC member, he was there when the general idea of a Presidential visit to Peking was discussed. But it would have been an easy thing to cable him twenty-four hours in advance of the announcement so that the Vice President wouldn't be caught wordless in Kinshasa. This the Nixon White House failed to do.

So why do American Presidents treat their Vice Presidents this way? In that particular case, the reason lay in residual White House distrust of Agnew's position regarding our growing relations with Mainland China. Distrust which was traceable to the incident of the Williamsburg Nine in 1971.

The Williamsburg Nine weren't New Left dissidents hauled into court by John Mitchell. They were nine reporters called into Agnew's suite one midnight to get an earful of his views regarding news coverage of the U.S. ping-pong team's trip to Mainland China. That was the historic trip that broke the ice on U.S.-China relations.

Agnew was attending a Republican Governors' Conference at Williamsburg, Virginia. On the Sunday we left Washington for Williamsburg, a story appeared in *The New York Times* covering the ping-pong trip. The Vice President felt the story was cloying in the way it covered the Red Chinese.

On boarding his Air Force Two Jetstar that evening, Agnew made a biting reference to the story. Then he fell silent for the remainder of the short plane trip from Washington to Williamsburg. It was a danger signal.

Agnew could be a man of chilling restraint at times and heated impetuosity at others. At Williamsburg that night, the impetuous Agnew took over. Suddenly, at 11:30 P.M., he wanted to talk to the press. Not a news conference, only "a dozen or so in for an off the record talk."

Something was wrong, or about to go wrong. No doubt about it. But when a headstrong principal gives way to his own impulse, a PR man might as well relax, draw his paycheck, and start making plans to pick up the pieces afterward. I could no more have stopped Spiro Agnew from seeing the press that night than I could have talked him into seeing the same group earlier in the same day.

He gave me fifteen minutes to round up the lucky

dozen. There was a frantic quarter-hour as I scurried through the corridors looking for newsmen. There were plenty around. But I knew better than to include anybody from the *Times* or *Washington Post* in the group. Not to mention *Time, Newsweek, Newsday,* CBS, NBC, ABC . . .

I had three-quarters of a dozen when the clock ran out. Exactly fifteen minutes after Agnew sent me on my midnight search, I escorted what were to be the Williamsburg Nine into the Vice President's suite.

Pete Malatesta and Roy Goodearle, Agnew's top political aide, joined me in taking drink orders. Then, seated in a plush colonial armchair with the press group circled around, Agnew began talking off the record. Like hell.

For all Agnew's running combat with the press, he knew how to handle newsmen when it suited his purpose. That night he wanted to let off steam regarding Nixon's China initiative. As Vice President, he couldn't criticize the initiative itself. But the *Times*' story offered him a target he could attack without appearing to go head-to-head against a major Presidential policy.

The off the record session began innocuously enough with a discussion of football and sports. It moved to such general topics as the Vice Presidency as an institution and the 1972 elections. Then, subtly encouraged by Agnew himself, the subject of news coverage of the ping-pong trip came up.

Agnew cut into the subject with a finely-honed axe. He spent no more than ten minutes on his ping-pong peeve. Just enough, he knew, to dominate everything else certain to be leaked from the midnight session. At about 2:00 A.M. the group disbanded.

The story was out by the time I ordered scrambled eggs at six-thirty the following morning. Naturally, at least two dozen newsmen who hadn't been invited to the midnight séance called or dropped by to tell me to drop dead.

The PR gaffe was laid at my door which, after all, is what PR men are paid for. Why not? I was the press secretary. Everybody knew Agnew detested news conferences, so if he held one at midnight, whose idea could it have been?

Jules Witcover, then with *The Los Angeles Times*, got the leak from one of the nine insiders and was ready to go with a story. Witcover, a fastidious reporter, asked for an interview with Agnew since he was going to quote him second-hand on a sensitive subject.

I took Witcover's request to Agnew, who turned it down flat. The Vice President was furious—on the record furious. Off the record, he was delighted. Now he had the best of both worlds. His discontent with ping-pong diplomacy was out in the open, which registered well with right-wing Republicans unhappy over the Nixon China initiative. Yet he hadn't publicly repudiated a Presidential policy.

Best of all, Agnew's ploy allowed him to blame his old bête noire, the press. Why, those deceitful bastards couldn't be trusted to keep their word. It might have been understandable if the story had broken six months later, Agnew said. But twelve hours? Outrageous. No, he wouldn't be whiplashed into putting off the record remarks on the record, just because some member/members of the press had violated an agreement.

Witcover went with his story, based on the recollection of one of the Williamsburg Nine. But when members of the midnight group, including two wire service reporters, asked to be released from the off the record commitment so they could give a first-hand rendition of what Agnew had said, he refused that, too. It would be, said, rewarding "the culprit."

This led to an absurd situation in which everybody in the press corps could write about the Agnew midnight session except the people who were there. By noon of the following day, special buttons were being worn by members of the press covering the Governors' Conference. They read: FREE THE WILLIAMSBURG NINE.

It had been a shrewd PR move on Agnew's part; he had the publicity he wanted. But asked by the White House how the unwanted publicity came about, he could blame it all on an untrustworthy member of the press. It just went to prove what the Nixon White House had always said: you couldn't trust those bastards.

John Scali was the principal Nixon PR operative on Chinese détente. The White House failure to notify Agnew of Kissinger's mission and the announcement of Nixon's trip to Peking was Scali's twist of the knife, retaliating for the Vice President's Williamsburg session.

Clearly, Agnew's pride had been wounded. Here he was the Vice President of the United States, on a worldwide trip, upstaged by the President's assistant for national security affairs. To aggravate matters further, the traveling press, increasingly restive about the absence of hard news, was filing copy describing the Agnew trip as a round-the-world junket and a waste of taxpayer money.

To say that we departed Africa for Spain with Agnew and his traveling press contingent on a collision course would be an error in tense. The collision had already occurred. All that remained was to assess the extent of PR damage. But the worst was still on the agenda: after collision comes backlash. Agnew couldn't respond to his White House antagonists. But the captive press corps, 35,000 feet above the African wilds, offered an inviting target.

As at Williamsburg, Agnew used a surprise news conference as the vehicle to vent his pent-up frustrations. Shortly after we lifted off the runway at Kinshasa for Madrid, he called me to the front of the cabin and told me to assemble the traveling press for an in-flight meeting. This time, it would be on the record. Again, as at Williamsburg, I sensed something was about to go wrong. The last thing Agnew's mood had indicated on taking off from Kinshasa was a desire to communicate with "those bastards."

"So they want *hard* news, do they?" he said. "I'll give the bastards something that'll have 'em bailing out over the Sahara to file their stories."

"What do you have in mind?" I asked.

"Well, for openers: suppose I say I'll resign unless the President visits Chiang Kai-shek on his way to Peking?"

Mike Dunn, the foreign policy adviser, and I looked at each other. Did he mean it?

"Never mind what I'm going to say," Agnew snapped. "Just get 'em together in ten minutes." Then: "You'd just try to talk me out of it anyway."

Reluctantly, I set up the public address system for an in-flight news conference. Agnew's "gut instinct" on how to get headlines was right. It was hard news that would be carried next to Kissinger's front-page space.

This was the news conference in which the Vice President praised the leaders of all the African nations we had just visited—Ethiopia, Kenya, Zaire—and went on to draw invidious comparison between their leadership and that of some "querulous" black leaders in the United

States. Vintage Agnew, in one of his impetuous moods. The comparison was sure to draw heavy fire from editorial critics back home. They would accuse him of a perverse form of racism.

Congressman William Clay of Missouri made headlines himself by accusing the Vice President of "intellectual masturbation," in "flagellating the poor and downtrodden." Now the traveling press had the substantive copy they wanted. But the PR problem was beyond repair: the image of the Vice President as Foreign Policy Expert had been totaled.

It remained only for Carl Leubsdorf, the Associated Press correspondent assigned to the trip, to catalyze a month of discontent, removing any remote hope of even a minor PR plus from the trip. It figured to be Leubsdorf.

An aggressive reporter of the pre-Mau-Mau school, Leubsdorf at work is one of the most abrasive and tunnel-visioned Washington correspondents any PR man could encounter. He also happens to be among the best wire service political reporters in the country.

In fact, if a School of Communications asked me to design a laboratory course for public relations graduate students—a test putting the student's professional abilities under ultimate stress—it would consist only of spending three days on the road with two correspondents: Leubsdorf and NBC's Jack Perkins.

First, the student would learn humility and self-restraint. Being called a shithead a dozen times a day tends to encourage those professional qualities. He would also learn how to operate with zero tolerance for deviation from hard fact, i.e., to pay the penalty for excessive euphemizing. But most important, if the student survived his ordeal, he would emerge with requisite appreciation of the fact that an abrasive, tunnel-visioned newsman pursuing a story can be disagreeable without being biased.

So there was Leubsdorf, swaying in the air cabin aisle somewhere over North Africa, waving a copy of our Madrid itinerary in my face.

"WHY?" he was asking, "WHY DIDN'T YOU TELL US AGNEW IS GOING TO SPAIN FOR FRANCO'S NATIONAL HOLIDAY?"

I looked at the schedule. "What day is that?" I asked.

"LOOK, RIGHT HERE!" Leubsdorf replied. "ON YOUR OWN GODDAMNED SCHEDULE."

There it was, all right: the Vice President would attend Spanish national holiday ceremonies on the anniversary of Franco's coming to power. Since the schedule had been drawn up by the foreign relations staff while I was wrestling with John Scali's Red China leaks, I hadn't been able to read it that closely.

"That's what it says," I replied. "So what about it?"

"SO WHY DIDN'T YOU TELL US?"

"It seems to me," I said, slowly, getting into the spirit of the conversation, "that we did tell you because, as you just pointed out, IT'S RIGHT HERE ON OUR GOD-DAMNED SCHEDULE!"

"BUT WHY DIDN'T YOU TELL US BEFORE! WHY DID YOU KEEP IT A GODDAMNED SECRET?"

"LEUBSDORF," I replied, now caught up in the full exuberance of the moment, "WE DIDN'T KEEP IT A GODDAMNED SECRET. I DON'T SEE THAT IT'S MY JOB TO FILL IN YOUR EDUCATION WITH NA-TIONAL HOLIDAY DATES. BUT IF YOU INSIST: JULY FOURTH IS AMERICAN, JULY FOURTEENTH, FRENCH . . ."

The end of public relations. We flew into Madrid in

full cry. The first thing I did after entering the Madrid Hilton was call the manager and ask for an immediate laundry pick-up for the traveling press.

THANKS-BUT-NO-THANKS DEPT.

On the day following Spiro Agnew's return from his round-the-world travels, he visited the Oval Office to give Nixon a personal report on his conversations with foreign leaders. Too bad, said the Vice President, the press didn't cover the accomplishments of the trip. Only the controversies. But what are you going to do?

Why, there's a lot we can do, said Richard Nixon. Tell you what. Why don't I put my top White House foreign policy PR counsel on just that assignment? Rosemary, get John Scali on the phone . . .

4. No Fair, You Peaked

There is a tide in the affairs of men which, taken at the flood, leads on to shipwreck.

> Author, in letter to Jim Dorais, explaining his resignation from the Shirley Temple Black account.

———◆———

Timing. Spiro Agnew called it his "gut feeling." I got the salary, $36,000 a year, and all the Air Force Two sandwiches and Screwdrivers I could consume (too few on a flight to New York, too many on the way to Palm Springs). Not to mention the impressive title of Press Secretary to the Vice President of the United States. But I always knew that my employer-client's No. 1 public relations counsel was actually located somewhere along his upper alimentary canal.

"Politics is all *timing*," he would say, explaining why, after eight requests, he was still turning down an interview with Mike Wallace. "I respect your professional judgment, but this isn't the right *time*. Maybe six months from now."

Six months later the answer would be the same. Agnew did well on television, knew how to use it, but had a love-hate relationship with the medium. He was impressed by TV's power to reach millions who were unreachable through print, but he was contemptuous of its superficiality and afraid of its potential for squeezing a public figure dry.

The overexposed television image of his Vice Presidential predecessor, Hubert Humphrey, wasn't far from Agnew's thoughts. TV coverage of his Des Moines and Montgomery speeches attacking the news media had made his name a household word. But in nearly three years I was able to wheedle him into only three national video appearances.

"You've got to pace yourself," he'd say. "This business is peaks and valleys. Ever since I first ran for office I've had PR experts, friends, other politicians banging on my ear. Do this. Don't do that. They'd tell me that unless I followed their advice everything would go to hell in a hand-basket . . . Well, I'm the one who has to *feel* it"— he'd tap his middle coat button—"got to *feel* it, right here. In the gut. This is a high-risk business. *I* take the risks. One day I'll go on with Mike Wallace. But not now."

Then we would switch subjects. All a PR man can do with a client who has mystical faith in the ultimate wisdom of his gut is to move on to whatever gastronomically productive areas are open to advice.

Whenever Agnew went into his gut-spiel I was reminded of the Hollywood story about Harry Cohn, the Columbia Pictures mogul. The one about Cohn's rating a movie's box-office chances by whether he shifted around in his seat during a preview showing. If he did, the show was in trouble.

"Just think," Herman Mankiewicz exploded on hearing that news. "The whole world wired to Harry Cohn's ass!"

Like it or not, all top-level PR advisers are wired to their paymaster's gut. Agnew was typical of clients in the upper echelons of the political and business power structure. The higher the client's status, the less he needs —or feels in his gut he needs—counsel about *what* he ought to be doing and *how* he ought to be doing it.

At or near the top, the malleable client portrayed by most fictional accounts of the PR game—that lump of clay waiting to be molded by the media master's hand—is non-existent. The young PR man or woman who enters the field thinking he or she is destined to play Pygmalion to some nebbish's Galatea is headed for an ulcer or a new, more satisfying line of work.

Jim Mahoney, head of the Los Angeles firm of Mahoney & Associates and king of the celebrity PR business, sums it all up in telling about his relationship with Frank Sinatra, his biggest name client.

"I come to him and say, 'Frank, how about an interview with so-and-so, an appearance on this-or-that show?' He just looks at me with those baby blue eyes and asks, 'Why should I?' So what do you say? He's right. Why *should* he? He doesn't need it like somebody down the line humping for a break. He's got it all. He can pick his own shots."

Frank Sinatra made his own break before he retained Jim Mahoney. Just as Spiro Agnew had become Vice President without my professional counsel. Yet even taking on a client before he achieves superstar status —doing the Pygmalion bit—makes no difference in the long run.

Why not? Because no man of power and/or celebrity, once that exalted status is achieved, will ever concede he's the creation of a man in his pay. The Big Man, especially the Big Man who's clawed his way up, will say, "I came up from nowhere, now I have all these smart bastards working for *me*." Never, "I came up from nowhere and I'd still be nowhere except for this resident genius who tells me what to do."

Of course, the PR business is filled with practitioners who think otherwise. One claims he "made" Barry Goldwater. Another used to claim (but hasn't been heard from lately) that Spiro Agnew was his particular lump of clay. And probably, somewhere in the subterranean PR enclaves of Hollywood or New York, some flack is around to tell us that without him Frank Sinatra would be running a bar in Passaic.

The power-behind-the-power legend persists as a professional myth. But contrary to what PR self-promoters would have us believe, client gut feelings—whether the client is a politicial, business, or entertainment superstar—remain the controlling factor in public relations success. From time to time, a PR pro may bring a nebbish near the top. He can't keep him there, however.

Where, for example, are George Mahoney, Glen McCarthy, and Julius LaRosa? Emphasizing the point: *who* are George Mahoney, Glen McCarthy, and Julius LaRosa?

Wherever and whoever they are today, let me remind you who they were: respectively, a politician, a Texas oil entrepreneur, and an entertainer, all of whom had the impetus of lavish PR in their efforts to reach the top of their chosen fields. None made it for long.

George P. Mahoney, no relation to Jim, was the political nebbish Spiro Agnew stepped over en route to the Maryland governor's mansion. A perennial candidate with money to burn, George Mahoney had just enough political sense to know he needed professional help with his image. He had read all the books and seen all the movies, not to mention the attractive promotional brochures put out by political PR firms.

George had it figured: given the modern science of mass manipulation, if he turned enough money over to image-makers and publicity geniuses there was no way he could lose.

One of the experts he hired during an early race for U.S. Senate was John Kraft, a leading public opinion pollster. Kraft, who worked with Lou Harris in the early Kennedy campaigns, was summoned to conduct a survey in depth on why Mahoney had lost every previous statewide election he ever entered. Kraft took the survey, fifteen hundred interviews probing the attitudes of Marylanders toward his client. Mahoney got his money's worth, though not what he had hoped for.

"George, it's as simple as this," Kraft reported back. "The people of Maryland just don't trust you. Read the results for yourself."

"What can I do about it?" Mahoney asked.

"Nothing," replied the pollster. "It's terminal."

John Kraft, who is now dead, was my favorite public opinion pollster. Again, that special quality: candor. But Mahoney didn't listen to Kraft. Like a patient in search of a physician who'll tell him smoking isn't injurious to his health, he hired other pollsters and PR specialists in election after election, to refurbish and re-refurbish his image. Yet, despite all efforts, the patient invariably died.

It's occurred to me ever since John Kraft recounted that story that if his erstwhile client had listened to him and retired from elective—or in his case, unelective—politics, Spiro Agnew would have found himself running against another Democrat in 1966 and the history of visceral politics might have been written differently.

Be that as it wasn't, PR or no PR, there are certain

ideas whose times never come, just as there are some stars whose gut feelings work well in one area but not in another. Ronald Reagan's conversion to politics is an exception to the general rule that success in one field of public entertainment doesn't guarantee victory at the polls.

My brief experience working as an outside PR consultant to Shirley Temple Black in her 1967 campaign for Congress left me with an indelible impression of the general rule.

I was brought into the Black campaign by the San Francisco PR firm of Whitaker & Baxter, the pioneer agency in the field of political PR management. W & B's origins trace back to the mid-1930s, when the original husband-wife team of Clem Whitaker, Sr., and Leone Baxter gained national attention handling major California campaigns. As a college student in the forties, I was intrigued by stories of the elder Whitaker's gut-cutting approach to his business.

"The average American doesn't want to be educated," Whitaker once lectured an audience of his fellow PR specialists. "He doesn't want to improve his mind. He doesn't even want to work consciously at being a good citizen. But there are two ways you can interest him in a campaign:

"First, most Americans love a contest, so you can interest him if you put on a *fight*. Second, most Americans like to be entertained, so if you can't fight, *put on a show!*"

A man after my own down-home Earl Long gut feelings. Unfortunately, by the time I arrived on the PR campaign scene, old Clem had passed on, leaving the Whitaker & Baxter tradition in the hands of his son, Clem, Jr., and three other San Franciscans—Jim Dorais, Mike Abramson, and Bob Smalley.

Smalley brought my skills to the attention of his W & B partners after the Goldwater Presidential campaign. While I served as Goldwater's assistant press man, Smalley was working as press secretary to the Republican Vice Presidential candidate that year, a man unremembered in history as William Who.

Adversity breeds close friendships. After we dug our way out of the November, '64 landslide, Smalley and I also shared a post-election public relations disaster. Republican party liberals were trying to oust Dean Burch from office. Burch had been Goldwater's choice as party national chairman. My contribution to the Save Burch effort was the ordering of two thousand pancake-size lapel ornaments featuring an elephant's head and bearing the slogan WE WANT DEAN.

Bad timing: twenty-four hours after my order came in, Burch traveled to Arizona, had a meeting with Goldwater, and announced his decision to resign the chairmanship without contest. There being no other candidates named Dean we could interest in the job (Rusk was a Democrat, Dizzy disinterested, and John at that time unknown), we were stuck with the buttons and a bill for $250.

But Smalley was impressed—bemused is a better word—at my effort to turn a dull intra-party fight into a button-wearing jehad. He saw me as both an expert visual gimmick man and quick gun at the typewriter.

So I ended up spending ten days in San Mateo, California, trying to help Clem Whitaker, Jr., and his partners wrestle with the nonpolitical viscera of Shirley Temple Black and her husband, Charles. That was all the time it took for me to conclude that the problem complicating the former child movie star's campaign, like George Mahoney's, was terminal—though not for the same reasons.

The public opinion polls indicated that our candidate had an astounding 98 percent recognition factor in the area. Her chief opponent in a special congressional election was Paul (Pete) McCloskey, a relative unknown at that point.

But the surveys revealed something else, too. Asked whom they intended to vote for, 12 percent said Shirley Temple Black, 7 percent McCloskey, 12 percent was scattered among lesser candidates, and the overwhelming majority was undecided.

The candidate and her husband mistakenly interpreted this as a portent of victory. She was ahead in polls, right? But when you have a candidate with a 98 percent recognition factor but only a 12 percent endorsement, it doesn't take a Jeb Magruder to know you have a little PR problem. It was the image of Shirley the Celebrity blotting out the desired image of Shirley the Member of Congress; the adorable child star overshadowing the would-be public servant who could best represent San Mateo's interests in Washington.

Charles Black, like his wife, is a decent, intelligent, civic-minded American out of his element in the political world. Nevertheless, he was rigid in his views of how the campaign ought to be run.

At the outset of the campaign, Black and his wife agreed they wouldn't let her participation in politics interfere with their family life or the amount of attention they gave their children. This decision translated into certain fixed rules during the course of the campaign.

Rule One: *The candidate will be home every evening for dinner with the family, seated around the table. No exceptions, for any reason.*

It was the kind of decision any decent, intelligent, civic-minded American would make. Which explains why more candidates of this type aren't elected to public office.

Politics in a free society, you see, doesn't have to be dirty, in the mud-slinging sense. But it can't help being disorderly. No political campaign is really "organized." All campaigns in fact operate in various stages of disorganization, like confused armies grappling in the night. Neat, containerized engineering and accounting minds strain against this chaos. They try to block out campaign days in clean lines and patterns. Such minds, alarmed by human variables, are the nemesis of every PR specialist who ever worked a campaign.

What I always hoped for in a political candidate was: (1) quickness, or the ability to set a fast pace and keep the opposition off balance; (2) an awareness of the essential fluidity of political campaigning; (3) a willingness to improvise; and, (4) a preference for the imaginative rather than copybook approach to each campaign day.

Unfortunately, most conservative candidates are conservative in their approach on how to campaign as well as their ideas about what to do if elected.

Charles Black has a conservative engineer's mind. This, combined with his wife's passion for familial order —a trait no doubt produced by those hectic years as a child star—dimmed any chance of our running a quick, fast-paced campaign.

The Clem Whitaker directive—give 'em a fight or a show—was doubly frustrated. The candidate wouldn't fight because her instincts were those of a decent, middle-class suburban housewife. As for giving 'em a show, that was out of the question. Shirley Temple Black's show-biz image was the problem, not the solution.

So here was the imported East Coast PR gun—on for $2,000 a month plus expenses—spending his morning at shopping centers watching his candidate get swarmed over by fans of little Shirley Temple. Yet he knew he was watching the very thing that would lose the election. Then, later in the day, Shirley would give a speech written by her conscientious, politically inexperienced husband: a good, sound-dollar speech, guaranteed to put even friendly audiences into stupor.

Pete McCloskey was shrewd enough not to pitch his campaign against Mrs. Black. He knew that his best PR weapon was the image of little Shirley Temple in a grown-up world. So McCloskey emphasized an overriding issue, the Viet Nam war (he was a dove, Shirley a hawk). He talked about Viet Nam in every speech, juxtaposing his image as a serious young Korean war veteran alongside his *"Littlest Rebel"* opponent. His weapon was gentle ridicule.

"I loved little Shirley Temple myself," McCloskey would tell audiences. The line proved devastating.

And so, while experts back East were peering myopically into New York and Washington crystal balls to predict Shirley Temple Black's landslide victory, Pete McCloskey established himself as the attractive alternative for whom San Mateo voters had been looking. He won the special election going away—a feat smart-assedly, but correctly described by one of his campaign aides as "the Sinking of the Good Ship Lollipop."

Running for elective office, Shirley Temple Black couldn't escape her image as a child star. But image transition can pose problems for working politicians within the trade. How many "new" Nixons were there over his twenty-eight-year political career? Yet the old, original image hung on with a vengeance, to the very end.

In former years other politicians have also sought to

undergo imagectomies. Staid old Senator Robert Taft, faulted as a national candidate for being too cold and detached, had PR experts like Jim Selvage struggling for years to humanize him as "Fightin' Bob" Taft. The effort fizzled because Taft's public style didn't make that image credible.

Then there are pols successful on one level of electioneering, but unable to develop a winning formula on another. Big Jim Folsom, despite being elected governor of Alabama twice, summed up that problem after taking a bad beating running for a minor party office.

"God has decreed I can only be elected to one office," said Folsom. "So be it."

And so it's been for Nelson Rockefeller, the most succesful politician in the history of New York State. A study of Rockefeller's career reveals the strengths and weaknesses of professional PR as a modern campaign tool, since no political candidate has ever used it as extensively. The results are mixed: spectacular success in state campaigns, equally spectacular failure nationally.

In 1958, when Rockefeller first ran for governor, early surveys showed him far behind the incumbent, Averell Harriman. Rocky's gut feeling and bank account told him otherwise, and his blintz-and-pizza-eating style of campaigning (he was the first in the field) clicked with a heavy PR/advertising drive and swept him into office.

Rockefeller was re-elected in 1962. But his 1966 campaign is the one that political PR-ad men around the country still cite as an example of what professional media work can do in overcoming a popular prejudice against a candidate's personal life-style.

Running that year for his third term, Rockefeller was difficult to market because of a combination of problems he had brought on himself. The most important of these problems was his divorce and remarriage. The divorce offended Catholic voters, while the remarriage alienated the menopause vote.

Rockefeller's PR/advertising specialists sought to divert attention away from Rocky-the-unpopular-man to the accomplishments of the Rockefeller administration. It was the original No-Profile campaign; the candidate's face was never seen on television. Instead, all Rockefeller audio-visual and print graphics, handled by the ad firm of Jack Tinker & Associates, focused on roads, buildings, and other services credited to his leadership. The hidden candidate-with-a-record won in a landslide.

I copied the No-Profile technique when handling the 1968 Congressional re-election compaign of Rockefeller's Cleveland cousin, Mrs. Frances Bolton. Mrs. Bolton had a solid twenty-year record of service in Congress, was a multi-millionairess, and had a ton of money to invest in her re-election drive. In addition, she was popular among her constituents.

That was the good news. The bad news was her age: eighty-three years old. She didn't sound eighty-three or think eighty-three, but on camera she looked it. The opponent, Democrat Charles Vanik, was also an incumbent Congressman, pitted against Mrs. Bolton in a redistricting shuffle. Vanik ran a hyperthyroid campaign, which aggravated our problem.

Our Bolton TV spot was modeled after Rockefeller's successful '66 package. We featured footage of hospitals, post offices, roads—everything stressing the Bolton contribution to the district. Rob Diefenbach, a film expert who wrote the first book on how candidates should make up for television, was brought in to produce a TV documentary.

Our film showed the candidate in quick, carefully filtered still shots. A voice-over commentary by the candidate gave the viewer the impression of Frances Bolton's presence on the screen, although the candidate wasn't actually exposed to the cameras.

Good soap-selling technique, but no soap. What worked for Rocky in New York didn't wash for his cousin in Ohio. Proving again that there are some disabilities that even the best-implemented PR techniques can't overcome.

One measure of Rockefeller's success as a candidate for elective office is that few people can now recall the chief obstacle in the way of his public acceptance in 1958. It was the very fact that his name was Rockefeller. There was a time when being wealthy could be the kiss of death for a man's (or a woman's) political career.

Candidates like Harriman, also a multi-millionaire and bearer of a surname not beloved by those who remember the Robber Baron period of American economics, helped pierce that image barrier for the rich and politically motivated.

But the election of the grandson of the Baron of Barons—old John D. himself—was an historic breakthrough.

After the election of Nelson Rockefeller as Governor of New York, the day was past when a rich candidate had either to hide or overcome the handicap of personal wealth.

To some degree, Rockefeller's success in 1958 dissipated the issue of John Kennedy's inherited wealth in the Presidential campaign of 1960. Just as Kennedy's election broke down the myth that no Catholic could win a national office.

Yet, successful as Rockefeller was in New York State politics, once beyond the state's borders all his PR horses and all his ad men couldn't win him the Republican Presidential nomination. Running for the White House, Rockefeller, the PR man's dream as a gubernatorial candidate, became a nightmare of poor timing, his gut instincts no better than those of a George Mahoney or Shirley Temple Black.

Rockefeller's technique for losing Presidential nominations was perfected early, in his very first attempt to snatch a Republican convention from Richard Nixon. That was 1960. The New York governor's three-stage formula for failure in national elective politics didn't vary through three elections over an eight-year period.

First, he jumped into the race too early. Then, for reasons incomprehensible even to his best political friends, he dropped out unexpectedly. Finally, his campaign organization dispersed and friends committed to other candidates, Rockefeller leaped back into the race, dollar machine at full throttle.

This sequence was launched for the first time when the now Vice President, seized by a gut feeling, chose Christmas Eve, 1959, as the quitting date for his 1960 campaign. He re-entered the contest half a year later—to the vast enrichment of his foredoomed PR/advertising counsel—only after Nixon had the nomination sewed up.

Again, in 1964, Rockefeller jumped into the Presidential race late, this time after Barry Goldwater had the nomination all but sacked. That year, however, the New York governor's own instinct for bad timing on the national scene was augmented when, on the eve of the California primary, the Goldwater candidacy was graced with a blessed event: "Happy" Rockefeller, the Governor's young second wife, had a baby. Goldwater won the primary by a narrow margin, this last-minute reminder of Rockefeller's remarriage having swung thousands of wavering voters.

Finally, again in 1968, it was Rockefeller versus Nixon, with the three-stage loser's formula a matter of routine. That year, Rockefeller dropped out of the race "unequivocally" in a major national television announcement. The decision caught his ardent supporter, Maryland Governor Spiro Agnew, unaware. It led Agnew into the Nixon camp, where he stayed—even after Rockefeller's unequivocal re-entry into the Presidential race at the Republican convention.

To a self-processed politician like Richard Nixon, Nelson Rockefeller's ins and outs must have seemed the vagaries of a spoiled rich kid. Nixon was the pure twentieth-century political mechanic, a programmed candidate whose only similarity to Rockefeller was his faith in the ultimate efficacy of campaign PR.

The problem with working for this kind of candidate isn't that the client doesn't understand what you're trying to do, as was the case with the Charles Blacks. It's that he thinks he *does* understand, and after his first campaign considers himself more expert in PR than his paid experts.

Nixon established himself as the final arbiter of all PR campaign questions, down to the smallest detail. In other campaign areas he might delegate authority, but not in the area of PR. He felt he knew it all. Given the slightest opening by a political visitor to the Oval Office, Nixon would deliver seminar lectures on PR technique and how to handle the press. All beginning with the line, "Now, when I was running for——back in——"

Despite his feeling that he was the best PR man in the business, however, Nixon's public relations instincts were actually those of a political wind-up doll. He had a lawyer's—not a PR man's—mind. And this cast of mind finally came to permeate the campaign atmosphere whenever he ran for office.

This was why so many of his campaign PR gimmicks

came off as heavy-handed and transparent—like the little Ohio girl in the 1968 campaign with the poster "Bring US Together." The girl was genuine, but everything else about the handling of the incident was contrived, like those precision-timed balloon drops that became the trademark of Nixon rallies.

Like Rockefeller, too, Nixon hired the best pros he could find in the audio-visual field for his campaign. His staff included film and video experts like Frank Shakespeare, Roger Ailes, and Bruce Herschensohn.

The former President's first great television success had been his 1952 "Checkers" speech. He had saved his place on the Eisenhower ticket with that one speech, and his concept of effective political TV was shaped by the experience. Gene Wycoff, in his book *The Image Candidates*, pointed out that thereafter Nixon always believed the surefire approach to winning votes via television was for him to "go on and talk to the people," without frills (save a bust of Lincoln here, a family portrait there . . .).

Audio-visual experts like Wycoff often urged Nixon to adopt more imaginative techniques in campaign television, along the lines of Rockefeller's 1966 gubernatorial race. But with one unforgettable exception—the climax of the 1970 mid-term election—the experts were always overruled by Nixon's preference for the "talking head" format.

That was the year that Nixon, after campaigning across the country on behalf of Republican congressional and state candidates for office, went along with an expert proposal (though not an audio-visual expert) that the final Republican vote appeal be a black and white film "documentary" production showing violent anti-Viet Nam war demonstrators.

The PR theory was that viewer-voters would be repelled by a raw presentation of long-haired violence.

These are the people opposed to the Nixon administration, was the documentary's statement. *Do you want this crowd running America?* The message for Middle American voters was clear: Go to the polls tomorrow and smite the "radiclib" candidates who are "soft" on long-hairs.

Nixon bought the package. But then a surprising thing happened. The network scheduled to run it—CBS, the administration's old bête noire—tried to talk White House advisers out of their theory.

CBS executives were afraid the production was so unprofessional it would repel viewers in a way its Republican sponsors weren't bargaining for. The network asked the President's staff to consider whether the film, as an election-eve vote bid, might do their cause more harm than good.

Nixon's campaign directors held their ground, believing the very rawness of the production would subliminally enhance the feeling among voters they sought. The Republican campaign committee's 1970 election-eve TV film was a masterpiece of audio-visual cacophony—erratic camera angles, over-exposed lighting, scratchy sound. All of which went before the American people election eve—back-to-back with a Democratic party-sponsored appeal by Senator Edmund Muskie in a quiet living room setting—just talking to the people.

Bob Squier, the Democratic campaign TV expert who handled the Muskie appearance, had decided on a simple "talking head" format for the Maine Senator as a tactical answer to what he believed would be Nixon's last-night appeal.

"I figured they'd go Oval Office to living room, with Nixon talking from a White House platform," Squier said afterward. "There was no way we were going to match that kind of show, so the best answer was to underplay for contrast. But I never expected *that* kind of contrast."

Nixon's campaigns were always an odd mixture of stultification and overkill. Overriding everything was the candidate's passion for order, a gut feeling left over from the defeat he suffered in 1960.

That year, in addition to the mistake he made in agreeing to television debates against John Kennedy, Nixon let himself be drawn into a frenzied cross-country footrace with his opponent. This was the Kennedys' game, the thing they did best. Only after he had played and lost did Nixon realize his error.

The result was that in later Presidential campaigns Nixon became obsessed with the idea of controlling the pace of his activities, down to the fraction of a minute. His fixation with "peaking" at precisely the right campaign moment (he believed his 1960 "peak" was reached two weeks too soon) suited the theories of organization-minded technocrats around him. These were the men who regarded a political campaign as an engineering challenge, subject to exact computation.

Not that political campaigns don't "peak." That is, they do achieve maximum vote potential at a particular moment. But given human variables, the question is whether this phenomenon can be charted and controlled.

Nixon tried to do just that in his 1968 campaign against Humphrey. This determination not to "peak" too soon resulted in a loss of campaign momentum. In the end, it almost cost the candidate an election earlier projected as a landslide win.

The most visible sign of the Nixon campaign *modus operandi*, however, was its penchant for detail. Even spontaneity was programmed, since *spontaneous* spontaneity might have presented the candidate with the sort of human variables that made him uncomfortable.

Or, in one notable case, non-human variables.

The incident didn't happen to Nixon himself. But it nevertheless resulted in a special section of the Nixon Advanceman's Manual dealing with the preparation of elephant mascots at Republican rallies. The book, drawn up by the onetime head of Nixon advancemen, H. R. Haldeman, was based on the collected experience of various Nixon campaigns.

Under *E*, for *Elephants*, the advanceman on his first assignment was cautioned that at all Nixon rallies featuring a live Republican mascot, the animal should be given a thorough enema and left unfed for a specified period prior to the candidate's appearance.

This directive was triggered by an incident that occurred on Chicago's south side during the 1960 Presidential campaign, when Nixon's Vice Presidential running mate, Henry Cabot Lodge, was on a platform delivering a major outdoor speech. Two minutes into the speech, the party's elephant mascot—who up to that time had been standing alongside the platform, comporting herself with proper Republican dignity—cut loose with a series of wild nature calls. Then followed another unscheduled number that scattered the host committee and first five rows of spectators. Lodge cut his speech short and headed for his campaign plane.

It was the kind of spontaneous political gut feeling with which no running mate of Richard Nixon's—especially a proper Bostonian—could ever have been expected to cope.

5.   Taking-a-Ride

To be a good public relations man, a guy must have had some experience as a press agent.

> Congressman Lester Wolff, former Coney Island
> press agent

———————◆———————

And again, timing. Ambassador-Designate Clare Boothe Luce was running late, wrestling Senator Wayne Morse around the marble floor of a committee hearing room on Capitol Hill. Meanwhile, a few blocks away, Senhorita Denise Prado, the sweet young Brazilian beanshell sent to Washington as the Pan-American Coffee Queen, was cooling her high pumps in a foyer at the State Department.

It was April 28, 1959, a day to remember when they write the history of flackery: Gold's first major product promo since coming on as an account executive with Selvage & Lee. The account they trusted me with was the Pan American Coffee Bureau, a hemispheric trade association—that's PR euphemism for international commodity cartel—made up of Latin American coffee producers.

This was Coffee Day of Pan-American Week. What do you mean you've never heard of it? Check the official

PR calendar. It's as revered an institution as National Sandwich week.

P-A Week is composed of seven days in April—a period celebrating all the wonderful progress made in hemispheric relations during the past half-century: you know, our transition from U.S. gunboat to Soviet missile-base diplomacy. Even under ordinary circumstances it's a grim social affair. But the 1959 edition was a special drag. Fidel had just come to power. He and his delegation were moving around all the inter-American meetings, being a general pain in the ass, while the Eisenhower State Department wrung its hands.

Me, I could have cared less. My problem wasn't to make Pan-American Week a success. Only Coffee Day. Let the State Department flacks worry about front-page stuff. All I wanted was sidebar space on a low-budget promotion. One photo of Denise Prado carried on back pages around the country and Selvage & Lee would have earned its monthly retainer (which I estimated at between $3000 and $5000 in 1958 dollars. They never tell account execs about client fee scales. You have to pry that out of a secretary.)

The challenge was to get the Coffee Queen together with any dignitaries we could euchre into a photo-session featuring raised cups of the client's product. To make this contribution to hemispheric solidarity I worked up a two-way promo designed to take-a-ride on a pair of evolving news developments: first, there was the admission of Hawaii to the Union; second, Clare Luce's appointment as Ambassador to Brazil.

Taking-a-ride, as the phrase indicates, means hitching onto somebody else's publicity wagon as it drives by. You harness imagination to opportunism and emerge with a gimmick like . . .

Passing out black eye patches, with the message GO BOB GO, to Pittsburgh kids in October, 1967. Ostensibly this shtick was only to make parents remember that Bob Friend, candidate for County Comptroller, had been a Pirate pitching hero during the 1960 championship season. But what I really had in mind was taking-a-ride on the Six-Day War, subliminally persuading the then-flourishing Moshe Dayan Fan Club that my candidate, although Republican, was their kind of goy.

Or what about sending in Batman to shut down a convenience food store in Birmingham, Alabama, on a Sunday morning? Here the idea was to take-a-ride on the popularity of a TV show to satirize the county's blue laws, thereby encouraging the state legislature to permit food sales on the Lord's Day. Funny? You should have seen the TV cameramen break up. But not, unfortunately, the legislators. Moral for PR students: if you're out to take-a-ride, satirizing the Lord's Day in the Bible Belt can be a bad trip for the client.

Or, on another sports kick (the national passion for jocks is the most commonly used PR vehicle going), what about my trying to hype up the grimy image of the American coal industry by taking-a-ride on "The Violent World of Sam Huff?"

I first met Huff in 1959, when he was middle linebacker for the New York Giants and had just been raised to national celebrity status by a *Time* magazine cover story and TV documentary. The documentary gave the American public its first close-up view of what pro football is all about.

My job was to promote the coal industry. A decade and a half before the Great Energy Crisis this posed a challenge to even the most imaginative PR man. Coal's image was that of a dying industry. My answer to the challenge was to hitch my client's decrepit image to something dynamic—pro football. Huff, straight out of West Virginia coal-mining country, was the vehicle.

To take-a-ride on the Giant superstar's fame, I proposed that the coal client sponsor a "Sam Huff Day" at Edna's Gap, the small West Virginia mining community where his family still lived. The event—really, an *eventoid*, since it was to occur for no other purpose than publicity—would take place a few days after the Giants-Colts championship game of 1959.

In a situation like this, the length of your PR publicity ride is contingent on the outcome of another, real event, over which you have no control. If the Giants won and Huff had a good game—say, sacking Johnny Unitas on camera a half dozen times—my "Day" at Edna's Gap could turn into a *Sports Illustrated* feature. But if they lost . . .

And of course, they did, in the fourth quarter. Right there before my bleeding eyes, *Sports Illustrated* turned into *The Charleston Gazette*. But still, an eventoid is an eventoid, and our Edna's Gap celebration of their hometown hero went through on schedule. The "colt-busting" saddle I'd arranged to give Huff (he bred horses in the off-season) would still make a good photo prop. And after a luncheon and photo-session we were to go down the twisting West Virginia road to Consol No. 9, where Sam would visit the coal shaft where his father and brother worked.

That last bit came as a surprise to the honored guest. He pulled me aside after the earlier photo-session to ask whether visiting the mine was absolutely necessary to make his "Day."

"Not absolutely," I told him, "except that the whole shift has been alerted that you're coming, you know? Besides, we've got another picture planned for down there. You, your father, your brother . . ."

"Thanks for the Day, but no thanks," said Huff. "Frankly, I don't want to go down into one of those things."

"Look, your skinny old man and brother do it every day," I said, taken aback by the timidity of this 230-pound living legend. "I mean, considering what you do every Sunday afternoon, what's going into a mine shaft?"

"You look smart, but you're some dumb," Huff replied. "I've been busting my ass in football since I was a kid, Charlie. You know why? *To keep from having to go down mineshafts.*"

Still, in the eventoid, Huff proved a trouper. He sucked up his gut and joined us on the trip into the bowels of the earth. But when the elevator finally returned us to the surface, the terror of NFL linebackers made a vow: never to do it again. Not even for a publicity stunt.

Huff was prescient: a postscript to this story is that in 1968, Consol No. 9 was the scene of one of the worst coal mine disasters in history. (No member of his family was in the mine at the time, however.)

Obviously, the PR man who's on the lookout for a publicity ride has to be single-minded. Solemn commemorations, wars, disasters, floods—to the working publicist, all such developments fit into a larger picture: how to exploit the situation for a client.

Exhibit: Ghetto walking. As a political campaign technique which takes-a-ride on poverty, the ghetto walk was all the vogue in the mid-1960s, before John Lindsay ran it into the ground pounding the streets of Harlem.

Before going to work for Spiro Agnew—whose disinclination to visit slums was well known—I choreographed a number of ghetto walks for politicians interested in demonstrating concern and compassion for the poor.

During my stay in Pittsburgh, for example, I was asked to develop publicity to point up a Democratic incumbent's failure to cope with rat infestation in poor areas. My gimmick was to create a "Rat Patrol" headed by Senator Hugh Scott, who flew in from Washington to walk the ghettos in search of rodents. We didn't find any, but no difference. With newsmen and TV crews trailing Scott, the phony "patrol" achieved its sole aim: the six o'clock local news.

In the commercial PR field, commemorations are always good vehicles for exploitation. Especially patriotic commemorations that identify your client or his product with God and Country. In this regard, the Bicentennial gives promise of being a veritable orgy of PR ride-taking and cheap commercialism. If I were still in the PR business, all I'd want would be the red, white, and blue paint concession.

Then, of course, there are natural disasters. Handled deftly, these also can be PR bonanzas.

Once I represented a Southwestern multi-millionaire with long-term political aspirations, who was searching for ways to overcome the handicap of his millions in a particular congressional district. We were in luck: two months after I went on his payroll, a tornado struck the area.

A hefty check to the Red Cross, plus food and blankets shipped in via private plane were obvious moves. But the client could have thought of those on his own. My professional touch entered when I persuaded him to perform

85

his philanthropy without fanfare. I advised that he insist on anonymity in all dealings with the Red Cross, which he did.

The Red Cross honored his desire for secrecy. Then, three months later, I leaked word to a friendly newsman in the area about my client's humanitarianism. The story was front-page copy—though it could have been smothered on page 3 in the immediate aftermath of the disaster. As I'd figured, my client's insistence on doing his good works without credit gave his contribution a genuine touch of humanitarian class.*

In case anyone has missed the point, as a ride-taking press agent I was blessed with a fair amount of requisite professional insensitivity. But nowhere near that of a client company PR vice president I was supposed to meet on the afternoon of November 22, 1963. We had a 3:00 P.M. appointment, but after news of John Kennedy's death in Dallas, I decided the question of how to handle the long-range PR problems of the plumbing industry could wait.

So I headed for the client's office, around the corner from my own, figuring to walk in, reset our appointment for the following week, then ask him to join me for a drink at the Carlton. The area around our offices, two blocks from the White House, looked like an outdoor shock ward. People were either wandering aimlessly or toward the nearest bar.

When I walked into the client's office, the PR vice president was just pulling copy out of his Remington

---

* For readers interested in such incidentals, I later parted ways with this client; he switched gears and decided to run for governor. As a millionaire Republican, he won his primary, but lost the election to a millionaire Democrat not particularly known for his philanthropy.

manual. He leaned across the desk before I could open my mouth and handed me the first sheet of a press release.

"Take a look," he said amiably. "Tell me what you think."

> *FOR IMMEDIATE RELEASE*
> *Washington, D.C. Nov. 22—What effect will the Presidency of Lyndon B. Johnson have on the middle-income housing market during the coming . . .*

"I think the company isn't paying you enough," I said. Then I headed out the door, leaving him to savor the compliment.

Of course, taking on a blue-ribbon prestige account sometimes means you have to reverse PR priorities. Sending Winston Churchill a case of bourbon on his first July Fourth as an American citizen is one kind of press agentry. But suppose you're retained to protect a Big Man's image? Then your job is to spot publicity hustlers looking for a free ride on your client's prestige. These hustlers come in two categories: show-biz and commercial product promoters.

As the Vice President's press aide, I was always alert to publicity hustles by aggressive show-biz flacks. I remembered from my younger days that one of the most notorious cases of taking-a-ride came at the expense of a Vice President. That was in 1945, when a Warner Brothers press agent perched a starlet named Lauren Bacall on Harry Truman's piano during a party at the National Press Club.

The picture, showing Bacall's cheesecake to advantage with a smiling Truman looking on, went around the world. It wasn't disastrous for the new Vice President, but it did contribute to an early general impression that Truman was an easily gulled lightweight operating in the heavyweight division.

Another memorable Washington press agent coup that saw a Big Man ridiculed by a show biz promo occurred in the 1930s. Financier J. P. Morgan was on Capitol Hill waiting to testify before a Senate investigating committee when a Ringling Brothers publicist stuck a midget on his lap. Lots of laughs, if you weren't Morgan's PR counsel.

Of course, you can always rationalize—as we used to when Spiro Agnew was annually beaning people with golf balls at the Bob Hope Desert Classic—that since such small things "humanize" a Big Man, they're a PR plus. But my professional instinct told me that the best PR "humanizing" didn't involve making the client appear the fool. Agnew, for all his public bonhomie about golf jokes, was of the same mind.

Having once been on the midget-planting side of press agentry, my inclination was to be hard-nosed whenever somebody tried to circus-hustle one of my Big Man clients. But there's a risk to that, too. A protective PR man can overreact while trying to make his principal flackproof. Which was what happened once when Dick Tuck, working for the Democratic National Committee in 1964, managed to slip a good-looking brunette aboard the Goldwater campaign train.

The girl's assignment was to get up at daybreak and slip an anti-Goldwater flyer called "The Goldwater Whistle-stop" under the compartment doors of traveling newsmen. My response to this planned subversion received national publicity, thereby violating the PR man's code of never getting your own name in the news.

Why overreact to a good-looking Democratic spy

circulating Goldwater spoofs aboard our campaign train? Professional pride. Dick Tuck had made a career of pulling off campaign stunts ridiculing Richard Nixon during his 1960 Presidential and 1962 California gubernatorial campaigns. After being alerted by friends in the press that Tuck was out to bug (in the old, pre-Watergate sense) the Goldwater campaign, I psyched myself into a knot, determined that my candidate wouldn't be snookered like Nixon.

Tuck's spy—at the time we didn't know whether It was animal, vegetable or mineral—made her first newsletter drop at sundown the evening our train left Washington. We had no idea how It had managed the job. Yet, somehow, traveling newsmen were breaking up over copies of the "Whistle-stop" when I dropped by the club car for a pre-dinner drink. The mimeographed sheet promised a second edition, to be delivered the following morning.

I got up at 4:45 A.M. figuring to catch It in the act. Almost too late, at that: Tuck's spy was already at work. I tracked the spoor of mimeographed sheets to a rear compartment where I came face-to-face with It, still carrying a bundle of flyers.

Tuck's spy proved to be a statuesque Irish beauty from Chicago, named Moira O'Conner. I later learned she was the daughter of the general counsel of Sears Roebuck, one of my real-life clients back in Washington.

As *Newsweek* accurately reported in the encounter, I was immediately struck with the enormity of my role in American Presidential campaign history and came on with a fair imitation of Humphrey Bogart nailing Mary Astor.

"I think you've made your last delivery, my dear." (It was a hard choice between "my dear" or "baby," but the hour of the morning seemed to call for understated irony.)

Then I threw my biggest client's daughter off the train at Parkersburg, West Virginia, with network cameras rolling and every traveling newsman and photographer on the train present to record the event. It was a tremendous victory for campaign counter-espionage. Next morning, however, I learned that Tuck had won after all.

The New York Times front-paged the story:

THE SPY ON THE GOLDWATER TRAIN
Girl Tossed Out into
the Cold for Issuing
Satirical Tracts

Parkersburg, W. Va., Sept. 29—"She was the spy," Timesman Charley Mohr led his story, "who was thrown out into the cold. A tall, pretty 23-year-old brunette was thrown off the campaign train of Senator Barry Goldwater into the damp, chill morning today . . ."

Toward the end of the story, Mohr reported that "Most male sympathies were with the willowy Miss O'Conner, and Mr. Goldwater's press secretary restrained Mr. Gold's crowing.

" 'It's a good story, all right,' said Mr. Wagner with a smile. Dropping his smile, he told his assistant, 'And, Vic, don't make it any better.' " So Tuck the prankster had his publicity. And I was left to ponder what should have been a proper PR response to Moira O'Conner's presence on the train. (Professional aside: despite the incident, I didn't lose the Sears account.)

Should we have ignored the spy? Invited her to dinner with Goldwater and staff? I still don't know. But the fact that this incident is the one most Washington newsmen recall about Goldwater's campaign travels tells us something about the dramatic suspense of the 1964 Presidential race.

I got to know Dick Tuck later and found him to be something more than the impish prankster generally depicted in the press. A shrewd press agent, Tuck is the prototype of a breed of anti-PR men skilled at diminishing public images.

On another occasion, during a Goldwater address to an open-air audience in Los Angeles, Tuck hired an advertising plane to swoop low over the area. My candidate paused in his remarks, looking skyward with his audience to read the streamer message (a take-off on the campaign slogan): IN YOUR GUTS YOU KNOW HE'S NUTS.

Wild antics. But after exposure of the Nixon campaign "dirty tricks" group in 1972, some White House supporters pointed to Tuck's operation as a precedent for what Donald Segretti was trying to do. However, judging from my own experience in '64, the Tuck and CREEP operations were different in one crucial respect: Tuck broke no laws.

Nevertheless, I think anti-PR press agentry—even when more prankish than malevolent—has no part in political campaigns. The question isn't simply what's legal and illegal. It's whether a campaign operation interferes with the opposition candidate's effort to get his message across to the voters.

This is to say that while Dick Tuck may be a very funny fellow, his gift for satirical press agentry could be put to better use than concocting schemes to rout an opponent's assistant press secretary out of the sack at the crack of dawn.

Although Spiro Agnew would have seemed an ideal foil for Tuck's operation, Dick and I never crossed paths during my years as the Vice President's press secretary. Instead, I was preoccupied with beating more conventional publicity riders at their own game. Commercial promoters like Colonel Sanders and Andy Granatelli.

Five years ago, the Colonel was the best product hustler in the country. Since then he's sold his chicken franchise and while still around, seems to have lost the old competitive zing. But in his day, given a celebrity and a cameraman at five hundred yards, that old chicken hustler could *move.*

Granatelli is cast from the same mold. He'll get himself invited to the Big Celebrity Event of the Month, whatever and wherever it happens to be. Then, before a Secret Service guard can move between him and an honored guest, Granatelli maneuvers his 250 pounds into position for another eight-by-ten glossy, to be suitably inscribed, "To my good friend, Andy, from . . ."

Strictly speaking, this is self-promotion. But in cases where a product is closely identified in the public mind with a personality, like the Colonel and finger-lickin' chicken or Granatelli and an oil additive, product and personal promo come to the same thing.

What distinguishes press agentry from first-class public relations in taking-a-ride, however, is an extra back-scratching dimension. A politician gets no racer's edge having his photo taken with Andy Granatelli. But if a product promoter can come up with a publicity idea mutually beneficial to all images concerned, then you've got a blue-chip PR project going.

Which is what I had on Coffee Day, 1959.

My first eventoid that day was scheduled for the Congressional Hotel on Capitol Hill at 9:30 A.M. A Hawaiian Coffee Break, first and last of its kind, "hosted" by Delegate John Burns of the Territory of Hawaii. Leis and orchids, but no hula girls. Not at *that* hour, with fifty

Senators, Congressmen, and foreign dignitaries expected to attend.

Sure, I'd considered it. But the problem was: (1) none of Burns' secretaries hulaed; (2) we couldn't afford to fly anybody in from Honolulu; and (3) the closest thing available—rejected after a brief initial impulse—was a Nationalist Chinese stripper working nights in a B-Girl lounge on Thirteenth Street.

After learning that John Burns planned to run for governor of Hawaii when the territory achieved statehood later that year, my hunch was that Burns would be interested in getting his name and photo in the newspapers back on the islands by any route other than obituary. I suggested that he front a pseudo-social event honoring the Coffee Queen.

There are about a dozen such eventoids in Washington every month, conceived by PR men and "hosted" by some Senator or Congressman willing to shill for a commercial publicity stunt.

The PR client pays the cost of the party, which may run anywhere from $1,000 to $10,000. The "host" gets publicity for lending his official prestige to a function that otherwise wouldn't be attended. (The guests, after all, are mere props for photographers.) In addition, there's sometimes an honorarium—anywhere from $500 to $1500 —given to the "host" to sweeten his incentive.

To create an eventoid, however, requires a certain amount of expertise concerning the publicity-seeking vagaries of available "hosts." Some, like Senator Vance Hartke, will go for anything short of greased pig wrestling if it means a wire service photo in the home-state newspaper. Others, like Senator John Sparkman, pose special problems.

Sparkman is a "sleeper"—since the passing of Tennessee's Estes Kefauver, the most notorious "sleeper" on Capitol Hill. You try to get Sparkman and other "sleepers" for stand-up functions only. If the eventoid is a sit-down affair the Alabama Senator can bring a conscientious PR man to colonic spasms by dozing off in the middle of the proceedings.

Will your "sleeper," the star of the show, wake up in time to smile for photographers? You're never sure. But Sparkman, who has a political sixth sense for approaching cameras, somehow always manages. He'll brighten up, smile, and go through whatever *mishegoss* the script calls for. Then doze back off until awakened by an aide when the eventoid is finished.

Another element to look for in asking a lawmaker to shill for a phony publicity function is the proximity of his next election. Members of the House, who run biennially, are in a constant state of campaign heat. But Senators, with six-year terms, aren't all as accommodating as Vance Hartke.

In this regard, the three types of Senators I always found hardest to book as "hosts" were: (1) the Senator just beginning a full term after an overwhelming election victory; (2) the old Senate Club member who's served so long he thinks he holds the seat by divine right; and (3) the lame duck Senator who's been involuntarily retired by the voters, is independently wealthy, and just doesn't give a damn about anything for the remainder of his term.

The nature of the eventoid itself can affect a politician's attitude toward lending his presence and/or name to a publicity hustle. PR shticks generally call for an actual physical presence. But pseudo-events planned for charity sometimes use only a come-on name.

When Robert Kennedy was a U.S. Senator, for example, his northern Virginia estate, Hickory Hill, was often used for charity and fund-raising dinners. Engraved invitations, at anywhere from $500 to $2,000 per couple, were always carefully worded:

Senator Robert F. Kennedy
and Mrs. Kennedy
Cordially Invite You to Attend
A Dinner at Hickory Hill
For the Benefit of

· · · · · · · · · · ·

Invitees would arrive only to learn that, while the estate had been turned over to charity for the evening, the Kennedys were nowhere on the premises. They had invited guests "to attend a dinner" not "to join them." A worthy shill. But nevertheless, many a National Capital social climber dipped into his bank account for a cause, thinking he and his wife would be able to say next day that they "had dinner with the Kennedys at Hickory Hill last night."

Even Presidents' names have been used for charity shilling. Carl Byoir, a PR pioneer, played datesmanship with Franklin Roosevelt's birthday on behalf of the Warm Springs Foundation, a national organization composed of polio victims.

According to Byoir, FDR called him one day in 1933 to ask PR help in promoting the foundation's work. Byoir recommended that fund-raising balls be held around the country on January 30, Roosevelt's birthday. Then, demonstrating pioneer chutzpah, Byoir took-a-ride on the pseudo-event he had just created. He slipped in his biggest commercial client, Henry Doherty, a utility and hotel magnate, as sponsor of the "President Roosevelt's Birthday Balls."

My game on Coffee Day wasn't charity, however. What I wanted from my low-budget, no-honorarium "host" was neither an estate nor a birthday. Only a live congressional body to smile, shake hands, and pose for photos with Denise Prado and whatever other visiting dignitaries could be lured into camera range. I couldn't use a Senate "host" since my promo was built around Hawaii, which had no Senator at the time. It did, however, have the only coffee-producing plantations in the United States, and that was all I needed to launch my 50th State publicity ride.

So Hawaii would be our first coffee-producing state! O.K., how does coffee-and-pineapple grab you? It seemed to me there had to be some traditional Hawaiian drink blending the two native products, and unfortunately, I was right. Stashed on my office bookshelf was a pristine, hitherto unopened copy of the client's recipe booklet, "More Fun With Coffee."

Have I mentioned single-mindedness as the dominant trait of the Compleat PR Angler? Proof of the principle: Why else would a flack who had qualms about palming off a Nationalist Chinese stripper as a hula girl serve fifty-odd Senators, Congressmen, and assorted diplomats the following concoction—at nine-thirty in the morning?

FROSTED COFFEE HAWAII

2 cups cold strong coffee
1 cup cold pineapple juice
1 pint soft coffee ice cream

Combine ingredients and beat thoroughly in electric blender until the mixture is smooth and foamy. Pour into tall glasses. *Serves 5 to 6.*

How do you say *fiasco* in Polynesian? The same way

you say everything else: *Aloha.* That, at least, was all John Burns was up to saying for an hour and a half as he smiled dutifully for the cameras through acid-pursed lips.

Our "host" did get his wirephoto in the newspapers back on the islands, however. And not long after, when Hawaii was officially admitted to the Union, he won the governorship he wanted, and deserved—if for no other reason than his game performance as Mr. Hawaiian Hospitality that morning. Draining not one, but two, cupsful of the hair of the PR dog that had bitten him.

In Portuguese, however, the word for *fiasco* is *fiasco.* I heard it several times, muttered by both my Coffee Queen and her Brazilian matron-chaperone while I sat in the jump seat of our rented limousine en route to Eventoid No. 2: a Coffee Break reception "hostessed" by Clare Boothe Luce, our newly appointed Ambassador to Brazil.

At the Department of State, I comforted myself, there would be no hokey concoctions. Only the client's legitimate product, hot and strong. But what I didn't bargain for that day was the culmination of one of the Capital's most historic mini-controversies, between two hot and strong egos.

Clare Luce, celebrated playwright and wife of one of the world's most powerful publishers, was the archetypal mid-century American male emasculator, verbally de-sexing her masculine adversaries when Germaine Greer was still pre-pubescent. Mrs. Luce, whose public and social personality seemed to be modeled on the film character generally portrayed by Katharine Hepburn, had just been confirmed as U.S. Ambassador to Brazil.

The chief opposition to her appointment had come from Oregon Senator Wayne Morse who, despite chairing the Senate Subcommittee on Latin American Relations, had only succeeded in delaying, not defeating, the Luce confirmation.

A few weeks before, I talked to the State Department's public affairs staff about ways my client and Clare Luce could help each other's images. Coffee being Brazil's No. 1 export and revenue source, I suggested that the newly appointed Ambassador share a Coffee Break with an attractive young Brazilian. In this country, the publicity edge would go to Senhorita Prado and the Pan-American Coffee Bureau. For Clare Luce, there would be wide-spread favorable publicity in Brazil.

Eventoid No. 2 was scheduled for 11:30 A.M.: a quick shutter session, no more than fifteen minutes. The traditional coffee cup toast, with cameramen lined up to catch the new Ambassador on her right, more photogenic, side.

But after our arrival at State, 11:30 passed, then 11:45. Very irregular. State Department publicity functions usually go off like Swiss clockwork. By noon, after briefing photographers for the fifth time on how the shot should be lined up, I began sweating the bullets of a publicist about to suffer the ultimate fiasco: a wash-out.

Suddenly my primary State Department press contact blew into the foyer, looking as if he'd just been given a new assignment to desk duty in the Orinoco delta. He summoned me into the corridor, away from my impatient Coffee Queen and the press.

"We have troubles," he said. "If Mrs. L. doesn't show in another fifteen minutes, it means a scratch."

"You understand, Lenny, that a cancellation *at this point* could mean my job," I said. "But if I'm *lucky*, all it means is my agency loses the account."

"*Your* job!" he giggled. A disconcerting reaction even from a middle-grade foreign officer. Then he turned and raced down the hall.

"Troubles," he had said. Leaving me to guess the worst. Which, in my frame of mind, could mean only that whatever the "troubles" were, they had something to do with me personally, or the morning's first fiasco.

Paranoia, you see, is the flip side of the egocentrism that afflicts all upwardly mobile Washington PR men, ages twenty-one to sixty-five. What, I wondered, had a modestly paid back-page item hustler done to alienate Clare Luce—without even meeting the woman?

Or was it something my Coffee Queen had done? Maybe a security problem. She was, after all, a foreigner in on a visa. Maybe they'd checked Denise out and learned that for all that upper-class Brazilian society front, she was actually a closet member of the Che Guevara Fan Club, Minas Gerais province chapter.

Then, mercifully, at 12:15—while the cameramen were packing their equipment and venting their thoughts about PR bullshit artists who kill half a day—SHE swept into the room the way only a Clare Boothe Luce or Katharine Hepburn can sweep into a room: brisk, well-groomed, and surrounded by a bevy of clucking young male assistants. She was all hard business in a chiffon package.

Let me admit it: I was awed. This, after all, was my First Celebrity, a Famous Personage in my immediate proximity (not counting sitting across a room from Charles Coburn at a war bond rally in 1943).

In later years, working around the White House compound, I would see the impact that Celebrity and Power, mixed in equal parts, can have on others. How a handshake with a Presidential candidate or Vice President can turn grown men and women into obsequious bowls of human jello. And I would recall that first encounter with Clare Boothe Luce, looking into her gleaming frost smile as I offered her a cup of hot black coffee.

"Mrs. Luce," I managed, "Senhorita Prado, this year's Coffee Queen from Minas Gerais."

The fixed smile stayed fixed as I went into a gambit designed to open small talk conversation between the two principals. You always try to get your photo subjects talking animatedly for the cameras, whether they've ever met each other before or will even remember each other twenty-four hours later. What the world has to see in a PR promo is smiling faces.

"You speak Portuguese, Mrs. Luce?" I asked. It seemed a good conversation opener. But suddenly, Clare Luce, who already seemed to be preoccupied, stiffened. The frozen smile melted.

"No," she replied, very clipped and Katharine Hepburnish, now looking through me. "I-do-not. Though-I-am-learning."

("You really made her day with that one," my State contact told me later. The new Ambassador's inadequacy with the native tongue had been a bone of contention about her appointment. But what single-minded back-page flack pays attention to that sort of detail?)

"Get it moving," snapped one of the Luce assistants, tugging at my sleeve. I stepped aside. The Ambassador and the Queen phased into stage smiles, while the cameras clicked and rolled. The session was over by 12:30, as per schedule. And if you're interested in historical PR trivia, you can check the next issue of *Newsweek* (the real triumph, understand, was that it ran in *Newsweek*, not husband Harry's *Time*). There in the right-hand corner of the Newsmakers page: "Clare's Last Stand." Because what the "trouble" had been around the State Department corridors that morning had nothing to do with a paranoid PR man or his client. It was Henry Luce's wife's doing, and hers alone.

For weeks, Clare Luce had remained mute under Wayne Morse's verbal assaults, while awaiting Senate confirmation of her appointment. There comes a point, however, when a woman—self-liberated before the term was even invented—particularly one with a penchant for skewering her male opposition, can take no more.

Once confirmed, her appointment now official, Clare was confronted by a mischievous newsman who asked her why she thought her confirmation had moved along so slowly.

"Oh, I would have been confirmed weeks ago," she smiled. "My difficulty, of course, goes some years back and began when Senator Wayne Morse was kicked in the head by a horse."

The story surfaced Coffee Day morning. As the Ambassador toasted the Coffee Queen, Wayne Morse, claiming a point of personal privilege, was on the floor of the Senate reading the wire service dispatch into the Congressional Record.

Now, technically speaking—that is, if the case had ever come before a court of law—the new Ambassador was on solid ground. Morse, a horse breeder, had actually been skulled by an equine several years before. But in the United States Senate, when the good name of a fellow Senator is involved, technicalities carry no weight.

Wayne Morse wasn't especially popular among his colleagues. No Senator in history, including Huey P. Long, had ever spoken to as many empty seats on as many varied issues. But he was a member of the World's Greatest Deliberative Body. And when a member of the Club is affronted by a non-Member who needs Senate approval for anything, neither *Time* nor *Newsweek* nor Holy Scripture can salvage the disaster. As of the moment that wire service story broke, Claire Boothe Luce's ticket to Rio was

No-way. Within a week she submitted her resignation and Eisenhower named a new Ambassador to Brazil—an appointee less likely to ruffle peacock feathers.

And that photo appearing in *Newsweek*—pulling bonanza from the jaws of fiasco on my first product promo —proved to be Clare Boothe Luce's final public appearance, at either a real or pseudo-event, as a member of the United States Diplomatic Corps.

FAST FORWARD SPEED:

Wednesday, Aug. 28, 1974
WHITE HOUSE SERVES NEW "MIXED" DRINK

Washington

They're serving a new drink at the White House these days.

"What's that drink?" President Ford inquired across the Cabinet room when he saw some of his economic advisers sipping an apricot-colored, iced drink.

"Iced tea and pineapple juice," came the reply.

—Associated Press

Ambassadors to Brazil come and go. But the American Coffee Break endures. Not by accident, either. It's one of this country's most successful ongoing publicity campaigns.

In the 1970s the coffee industry is faced with new threats to its hegemony over the mid-morning habits of Americans. Questions are being raised by doctors and consumerists about the effects of excessive coffee-drinking on the human heart. The industry's PR men are scouring lists of cardiovascular specialists in search of experts who, given the incentive of fat research grants, can come up with answers that won't depress coffee futures.

But back in the innocent 50s and 60s worries about *other* people's heart attacks were light-years removed from our thinking at Selvage & Lee. All we worried about then was tea-and-surpluses.

Iced tea's summertime bite into coffee sales was the reason Denise Prado had come to Washington. Each spring and summer a rival promotional association, the Tea Institute, along with its individual company members, launched a PR-advertising campaign to lure Americans into deserting our product for theirs.

The Coffee Queen's visit to the United States was the beginning of our seasonal counter-promotion. In addition to Coffee Day, we also tied the product into a safety-on-the-highway campaign during the spring and summer months. National highway safety groups were urged to advise drivers to pull over to the side of the road for a cup of coffee when they grew weary behind the wheel on holiday weekends.

This was more than fluff. The stability of a dozen Latin American countries, geared to one-crop coffee economies, was directly related to how many coffee beans were consumed in the world's biggest coffee-drinking country, the United States. Even the campaign urging American housewives to make their husbands happy by making their coffee *stronger*, while superficially a matter of gastroesthetics, tied into the overall program of greater bean consumption.

Given this background, the significance of the Coffee Break is clear. Diminish the sales of the client's product-and-Danish by 20 percent in a fifty-block radius of Manhattan alone, and the Monroe Doctrine would go down the tube. At least, that was the higher purpose that sparked us on. (What happened to Denmark and NATO was some other agency's problem.)

Other projections back then were even more ominous. Statistics showed that Latin American population kept increasing by quantum leaps. No matter how many ways the various Central and South American governments tried to induce growers to diversify crops, the coffee bean surplus swelled year after year.

Looking into a crystal ball from the perspective of Coffee Day, 1959, all our Coffee Break promos were of limited long-range value. By 1980, the average American secretary would have to drink twelve to fifteen cups a day just to save Uruguay, let alone Brazil, from joining the Third World.

Obviously, some external means of controlling coffee output, and maintaining price levels for our coffee plantation owners-clients, was the answer. For that, however, a different kind of public relations—one concerned with more than just getting photos into national news magazines—is necessary.

6. Integrity, Where Is Thy $ting?

The basic element of good public relations for any business or institution is integrity. Without it, there can be no successful public relations program.

Richard Darrow, *Public Relations Handbook*

———————◆———————

Sure, Dick: it isn't the money, it's the principle. But if that's the case, whatever happened to the "Red Menace" and "Cold War" American industrial leaders were pounding their rostrums about, only a decade ago? First chance they had to make a buck selling goods in Communist markets, "free enterprise" businessmen turned 180 degrees and put their speechwriters to work grinding out clichés about "détente" and "peaceful coexistence."

The fact is that American business, the body on which professional public relations feeds, isn't interested in ideological verities. Only profit-and-loss statements. PR men reflect that non-philosophy. They're retained to cosmetize client self-interest with whatever clichés are selling at the moment on an open market of pre-packaged ideas.

Offered a sufficient fee, most American PR firms will hire out to anyone. Provided that, in taking on an account, the agency doesn't lose other business, with bigger fees, in the long run.

Consider the case of Adolf Hitler's short-lived investment in American public relations.

In the early 1930s the new Nazi government, interested in luring visitors to Germany, hired Carl Byoir (remember the Franklin Roosevelt Birthday Balls?) to handle its tourism program in the United States. Byoir was a Jew. He came to the German account on the rebound from representing the dictatorial Machado regime in Cuba.

The Byoir agency's agreement with the Machado government—$60,000 a year for five years—had terminated abruptly for reasons all too common to PR firms specializing in Latin American accounts: the client was run out of office (by Fulgencio Batista, who hired a new U.S. PR agency). But Byoir's economic loss was relieved somewhat by the German contract, which ran $3,000 a month for a year and a half.

In later years, Byoir explained his PR tie with the Nazis by saying that back then, in the early 1930s, there wasn't any indication of what Hitler had in mind for the Jews. Only *Mein Kampf*. But the PR man probably figured that the book, along with der Führer's fulminating anti-Semitic speeches, was just so much empty rhetoric. Along the lines of what PR men spin off for politicians in this country.

The usual rationale for taking on a bastard account is that the PR ethic parallels that of the law. Lawyers take unpopular cases because every citizen is entitled to his day in court. PR men claim they handle "misunderstood" clients because every interest has the right to be represented before the "court" of public opinion.

Superficially, the parallel seems apt. But on close examination, it breaks down. The difference is that when they enter a courtroom, even the most predatory members of the legal profession are bound by rules of evidence. On the other hand, the "court" of public opinion operates like the Law West of the Pecos. Rules are rough-hewn, and truth can get ground into the barroom sawdust at the drop of a phony front-group or unattributed news leak.

Cleaning dirty laundry for foreign interests is a glaring example of how professional PR sometimes operates in an ethical gray area. Some foreign tourist and commercial accounts are benign. But other foreign clients hire PR representatives to work at influencing U.S. Government policy and public opinion along controversial, if not legally questionable, lines.

In past years, the most lucrative of these foreign accounts came out of Latin America, with sugar and coffee-growing interests the big-paying clients. More recently, the Arab countries, seeking improved "understanding" of their position in the Middle East, have spread oil on the Washington PR waters with a lavish hand.

PR fortunes were made representing South and Central American countries under the old Sugar Act. The Act set import quotas in the United States for sugar-producing countries. Its purpose was to protect our native sugar beet and cane growers and the quotas were a form of agricultural subsidy for U.S. farmers.

They were also a form of subsidy for National Capital PR agencies and lawyers, since the scramble to get quotas for individual Latin American countries proved a mother lode of six-figure fees. When the Eisenhower administration cut off Castro Cuba's sugar quota, for example, other Latin American countries were eager to take up the slack by having the Congress increase their own quotas. The ensuing activities of PR operatives to influence key Congressmen on behalf of foreign clients had to be seen to be believed.

But, of course, it's never seen. At least, not the most effective lobbying. This, after all, is an area of public relations in which success isn't measured by media space. The last thing a PR lobbyist working a foreign account wants is publicity. Staying clear of publicity is, in fact, the only way to play the subtle game of lapel-stroking.

I was never really worth a damn at stroking congressional lapels. Luckily, Sam Bledsoe, the head of Selvage & Lee's Washington office, was a great believer in two-platoon specialized public relations. He left me to my typewriter and press contacts.

Sam knew the danger of working outside your field of PR specialization because he himself had once been singed, venturing into the area of gimmickry on behalf of a foreign client. The incident occurred before I went to work at Selvage & Lee. It involved trying to con columnist Jack Anderson into buying a phony, albeit harmless, story about a sherry-drinking parrot.

One of the agency's clients was the Spanish Sherry Institute. The promotional side of the account was handled out of New York, and the Washington office was assigned the job of holding the Spanish commercial consul's hand if a PR problem developed along diplomatic lines.

The jealousy that exists between New York and Washington branches of the same PR agency sometimes gets intense. Sam, who is fairly intense without any provocation, thought the New York office didn't appreciate how much Washington was contributing to the account. So he and Duncan Waterman, my predecessor at the agency, devised an elaborate hoax involving a parrot—allegedly two hundred years old—that was kept alive by drinking a quota of Spanish sherry every day.

According to the story—instant legend, concocted by Waterman—the parrot had originally belonged to an eighteenth-century Spanish freebooter. The bird, said Waterman, had been passed along from owner to owner through the centuries and somehow ended up the property of a Spanish restaurateur in northwest Washington. A fake certificate of ownership contained a clause directing inheritors of the parrot to feed it a daily ration of Spanish sherry. That, said the phony document, was the secret of the bird's longevity.

Waterman, fluent in Spanish, painstakingly scrawled the deed on parchment, then soaked it in coffee to provide an aged, scrollish look. Then he borrowed a parrot from the Pan-American Union and spent two solid weeks teaching it to screech "Jerez!" and swallow sherry from an eyedropper.

Finally, Waterman turned parrot and parchment over to the restaurateur, who was hustling publicity for his own establishment. Duncan spent another day drilling the bird's new owner on how to handle press questions about the rara avis who had discovered the fountain of youth in a wine bottle.

The story was hokey, but it had a chance. Hokey stories sometimes sell because they're transparently hokey. Jim Moran, the Hollywood flack, works on this premise. When he calls the news media to let them know about a breaking story, everybody knows it's a ringer. But the fun lies in reporting the fact that a hoax is taking place. Moran doesn't care. Just so they get the title of the motion picture right.

But after all their elaborate preparation, Sam and Duncan, amateurs at that sort of flackery, made two critical mistakes which blew the hoax.

First, instead of breaking the story generally, they gave it a test run. Their thought was that if the story could con one reporter and he broke it, they would then follow up with a full-scale news conference. This would be a first: A National Capital news conference for an alcoholic parrot clearly identified as such.

So who do they call in? The Washington editor of *Parade,* the mass-circulation Sunday supplement, who, in another life, also happened to be Drew Pearson's top aide and the sharpest investigative reporter in the country. A fellow by the name of Jack Anderson.

It took Anderson no more than three questions (and a whiff of manuscript coffee) to reduce Waterman's carefully-coached restaurateur to a blubbering heap. He spilled the beans about the hoax and provided Anderson with a detailed account of Waterman's preparations.

Anderson was half-furious, half-amused. He called Bledsoe and threatened to run the story as an exposé of phony PR. Bledsoe was delighted. But then Sam made his big mistake.

"You run that story," Sam told Anderson, "and I'll see to it you get a full year's supply of all the Spanish sherry you can drink."

For that one, Anderson, incorruptible and Mormon, wreaked his worst vengeance. He never printed a word about the phony sherry-drinking parrot.

"Always be yourself in this business," Sam would advise after recounting that story. "There's a place for honest phonies in this town."

So I kept clear of lobbying because it wasn't my forte. It seemed an arcane business. While I had absolute confidence in my ability to cope with any publicity challenge, the sight of an expert lapel-man wining and dining a powerful committee chairman at Paul Young's restaurant left me guessing at how the conversation ran when they got down to serious business.

As a publicity flack, my technique would have been to get straight to the lead of my story: "Senator," I might have said for openers, "about that sugar quota you're holding up . . ."

That was *not* the way things were handled, I gathered from talking to the PR lapel-men working in the office. Instead, a special rapport helps these relationships along. The PR lobbyist doesn't need strong leads because wheeler-dealers understand each other by nuance.

Successful lobbying is an osmotic art. Which is why Senators and Congressmen themselves make the best lapel-men and are snatched up by PR agencies and trade associations when they retire voluntarily or involuntarily from Capitol Hill. It takes one to work one.

Anyway, back to sugar and coffee. Despite the fact that they both come from Latin America, these two commodities operate on different lobbying frequencies. The reason is that aside from Hawaii's minor annual production, no domestic U.S. coffee-growing industry exists requiring protection from foreign imports.

When the price of sugar is down, powerful members of Congress are eager to prop it up so that their beet- and cane-growing constituents are kept happy. But a drop in coffee prices because of a world glut doesn't raise any stir on Capitol Hill, no matter what the economic repercussions in Latin America.

Only when coffee prices increase do Congressmen sit up and take notice. Then they raise hell about foreign producers screwing the American consumer—the same consumer getting screwed by high sugar prices artificially created by the same Congressmen.

This was what happened in the mid-1950s, when Selvage & Lee represented Latin America's coffee interests in the United States. Coffee prices had skyrocketed. American housewives were sending threatening letters to Congress. In a full congressional session, a committee investigation was inevitable. Senator Guy Gillette, a liberal Democrat from Iowa, seized the moment and became the head of one.

The Gillette committee's final report on coffee prices was a PR debacle for Selvage & Lee's clients. It charged that the market price of coffee was being controlled by an international cartel. Of course, it didn't take a congressional investigation to determine that. Any half-assed burro plodding a trail in Minas Gerais province knows coffee prices are fixed. But the report went over great in the boondocks, which was all that interested Gillette. Like most congressional committee chairmen conducting investigations, the Iowa Senator was satisfied to get a few weeks' headlines, file a report that would gather dust, then move on to another field.

In defense of Selvage & Lee's handling of the Gillette investigation, let me say that there's actually very little a PR agency can do to protect a client from the ravages of a publicity-hungry congressional committee. The only two witnesses who ever walked into hostile congressional committee rooms and carried the day were Howard Hughes in 1948 and Frank Sinatra in 1972. More about the Sinatra episode later.

The problem the PR man faces trying to prepare a witness for a hostile congressional committee is that the men running the game hold all the publicity cards. You can rehearse a witness for days, but a clever committee member who knows how to play to the cameras and press table can leave your client cut and bleeding.

For some reason, probably having to do with the native waters, Tennesseans are born with special skills at milking congressional committee hearings for maximum publicity. Estes Kefauver anticipated Joe McCarthy by several years in his uncanny ability to work a headline a day out of a committee hearing.

Kefauver first crashed the national political scene as chairman of the Senate crime-investigating committee during television's infancy. His appearance and style resembled Henry Fonda during his *Trail of the Lonesome Pine* period. Senator Kefauver was the best publicity hawk in modern history; better than Joe McCarthy, Hubert Humphrey, Ev Dirksen, John McClellan, Sam Ervin, and the Kennedys.

Kefauver's strong point as a self-publicist was that he didn't *look* like he was hawking, which is where most egocentric politicians expose themselves. But Country Boy Estes, with his down-home Tennessee drawl and barnyard smile, seemed the most self-effacing person who ever shuffled into a committee hearing room. It was all calculated image-projection. Kefauver worked hard perfecting his country boy act for over twenty years and twice came close to winning the Democratic Presidential nomination with it.

Once I traveled south with Kefauver on a commercial flight. We were headed for the same event in Memphis, though not together. As soon as he got into his seat at Washington's National Airport, the senior Senator from Tennessee slipped on sleeping shades and was off to his reveries.

The plane made one stop, in Knoxville. I left my seat to get a magazine at the back of the plane. Looking out the window, I spotted a delegation of about two dozen Japanese businessmen on the landing strip, just arrived from the West Coast as part of a special trade mission sponsored by the State Department.

I couldn't have taken more than a minute selecting a magazine, but when I returned to my seat, Kefauver was missing. Where could he have gone? Not the men's room; that was next to the magazine rack. Then I took another look out the window. Guess who stood smack-dab in the middle of that Japanese trade delegation, having his picture taken for the Knoxville papers?

Five minutes later, eyeshades in place, Kefauver was asleep again, en route to Memphis. But as far as his Tennessee constituents who read the Knoxville paper would know, their Senator had visited the city and met with a visiting foreign delegation to discuss U.S.-Japanese trade relations.

In preparing a business witness scheduled to go before a Kefauver-headed committee, the best that any PR counsel could do was help the witness cut his losses. The bigger the business, the bigger the losses. Kefauver, a mid-South populist, spent the last years of his life investigating various major industries.

I remember the Tennessean presiding at the committee table, his eyes at quarter-mast, a canary-eating smile on his face. You could set your watch by him. Twenty minutes before deadline for the Eastern Standard Time final afternoon editions, Kefauver would drop whatever publicity bombshell he had planned for the day.

Once, during a Kefauver investigation of the drug industry, the president of a pharmaceutical company was secretly alerted by a committee staff member that the chairman was going into the subject of drug industry profits the following day.

Forewarned, forearmed. The witness, his lawyers, and a clutch of industry experts worked through the night preparing a detailed explanation of the economics of drug manufacturing, i.e., the cost of research, profit ratio, etc. The firm's Washington PR counsel looked forward to shoving Kefauver's questions down his throat. An artist was kept overtime in an adjoining hotel room reducing complex statistics to graphic charts for the greatest visual impact.

Next morning, as predicted, Kefauver dropped the big question. How, he asked the witness, could the drug industry justify its high mark-ups? The charts were pulled out, the easel set up, and the witness launched into his explanation.

It was one of the most thorough jobs of industry preparation for a committee hearing in congressional history. Kefauver listened, the canary-eating smile fixed. For a while he actually seemed impressed.

When the witness had finished (twenty-five minutes, with the charts), Kefauver began shuffling through a clutter of papers on the committee table. He mumbled appreciation for the witness' thorough recitation on the subject of drug pricing.

Then, his paper-shuffling routine having sufficiently lowered everyone's guard, the chairman proceeded to launch into a low-key, impassioned speech on the cruelty of "outrageous" business profiteering at the expense of the aged and infirm "who can't afford the medicines they need."

Guess what part of the committee hearings made the news lead that afternoon and next morning? The experience taught me a lesson: never ruin a good night's sleep trying to beat a publicity pro at his own game.

Ross "Big Mouth" Bass was another Tennessean

with a talent for brushing aside extraneous detail to get at the heart of a congressional committee investigation: publicity. When Kefauver died, Bass replaced him as Senator until the next election when yet another talented committee performer, "What-and-When" Baker, in turn defeated him.

"Big Mouth" was so-called to distinguish him from a quieter congressional colleague, Perkins "Small Mouth" Bass of New Hampshire. "What-and-When"—Senator Howard Baker—earned his nickname by looking soulfully into the camera during the Senate Watergate hearings of 1973 and repeatedly asking witnesses, "*What* did the President know, and *when* did he know it?"

While neither could hold a strobe light to Kefauver in garnering publicity from committee hearings, Baker was by far the smoother of his successors in carrying on the Tennessee tradition.

My one encounter with Bass came when he was a member of a House committee looking into the Billie Sol Estes scandal back during the Lyndon Johnson years.

Estes, once a Junior Chamber of Commerce "Man of the Year," had fleeced Texas farmers out of millions of dollars through sales of nonexistent anhydrous ammonia fertilizer tanks. Billie Sol was an independent contractor, but the company he represented—Commercial Solvents—was a respectable New York-based chemical firm.

Company officials claimed that Estes operated his fraud without its knowledge. When called to testify before a House subcommittee investigating the scandal, they came to Selvage & Lee for PR counsel. I was assigned to the account.

"Big Mouth's" technique of dominating a hearing was cruder than Kefauver's, partly because Bass didn't occupy the subcommittee chairmanship and had to flail for attention. But the result was the same.

Our witness was Maynard Wheeler, Commercial Solvents' board chairman. Like most businessmen, he was completely out of his element in Washington, and no match for the likes of "Big Mouth."

Bass would reel into the room ten minutes into the day's testimony, interrupt the proceedings to conduct a ten-minute harangue on the Evils of Wall Street, then storm out, winking at the press table as he left. Not only was the witness' testimony buried, but so were the more probing questions asked by sober-minded members of the subcommittee.

In time, "Big Mouth" was relieved of his Senate duties by Tennessee voters and went on to bigger and better things, lobbying his old colleagues in Washington. But the distinguishing characteristics of congressional investigations—whether a McCarthy, a Kefauver, or a Bass is the questioner—are the same: no matter what the issue, they produce more heat than light.

This was true of the Gillette committee investigating coffee prices in the mid-1950s. Twenty years later, coffee prices are still high—even higher—and for the same reason: they're controlled.

But now as then, if they weren't: (1) coffee would go two cups for a nickel at every Chock Full o' Nuts in America; and (2) the Senate Foreign Relations Committee would be conducting investigations to determine why a dozen Latin American countries had overthrown their governments inside a six-month period.

One of Selvage & Lee's assignments was to create a climate of opinion in which American consumers would understand the connection between coffee pricing and hemispheric stability. It was what we called a last-ditch account.

Selling the public on the idea that high prices are good for you is the next thing to pushing cancer as a way to solve the problem of overpopulation. No PR agency has been handed that assignment yet. But if one ever is, the outfit most likely to get the account would be Hill & Knowlton, the world's largest PR firm and undisputed king of last-ditch accounts.

Most agencies acquire clients in trouble; H & K gets rich on terminal cases. In recent years, with industry under continued attack from Federal agencies and consumer groups, Hill & Knowlton's operatives can be seen in Capitol Hill corridors and editorial offices, struggling against a *Zeitgeist* of distrust for their oil, steel, and tobacco clients.

Since the mid-1960s, H & K's campaign on behalf of the tobacco industry has been a model in terminal account techniques. Faced with a growing demand for government action to curb cigarette advertising, the tobacco industry reacted by creating one of the lushest PR funds in history.

When industry was attacked in Commodore Vanderbilt's day, its leaders could afford to circle the wagons and say, "The public be damned!" Modern businessmen, however, are responsible to broader segments of the public, including sensitive stockholders. In terms of substantive industry policy, the public can still be damned. But under advice of PR counsel, latter-day Vanderbilts are more apt to say, "The public doesn't understand."

Hill & Knowlton's first move toward improving public understanding of its last-ditch tobacco account was to form the Tobacco Research Institute. TRI is an industry-subsidized research and lobbying organization that operates out of Washington, D.C.

This kind of operation is different from phony "front" groups in which ostensibly independent grassroots organizations are secretly subsidized by the client. With TRI, the tobacco industry's financial support is out in the open.

The activities of phony PR fronts are varied. Some are formed for single-shot duty—say, an advertisement in *The New York Times.* Others are letterhead groups with stationery boasting prestigious names. They're established for full-blown propaganda campaigns, complete with computerized letter-writing to Congressmen and news editors around the country. Or, in heavily funded campaigns, a mass descent by "grassroots" lobbyists on Capitol Hill either to push or defeat particular legislation affecting the client.

Phony front groups can be spotted by telltale clues in their organization titles: words like *Fair, Independent, Consumer,* and *Citizens.* This isn't to say that *all* organizations containing those words in their titles are phony, only that nine out of ten phony front groups use them. The tenth uses either *Public* or *Emergency.*

Front groups provide a special-interest client with a facade of grassroots support. The organization may actually consist of three people on the PR agency's payroll, stashed in a closet with a mimeograph machine and a telephone. But to an unknowing Congressman or editor, the Emergency Independent Citizens Committee for Fair Consumer Practices is a nationwide organization composed of tens of thousands of concerned Americans.

This isn't the Tobacco Research Institute's *modus operandi,* however. TRI's purpose is to provide a steady barrage of medical-scientific data to counter evidence that cigarette smoking is a leading cause of lung and throat cancer, regardless of what the Surgeon General of the United States or your family doctor may say.

Sophisticated modern PR firms don't deal in generalizations about free enterprise versus socialism. That theme, while effective thirty years ago, falls on deaf ears in the 1970s. Instead, "research,"—in the form of statistics and other weighty academic data—is advanced to provide a client's case with "substance."

No matter how heavy the weight of evidence to the contrary, a resourceful PR agency with lines into academe can always find Ph.D.s or M.D.s willing to contribute their professional expertise to the cause of scientific research. Prestige of this kind can be bought in the form of industry-subsidized grants, for anywhere from $10,000 to $1 million.

Not that anybody with a doctorate would pervert the spirit of free, objective inquiry. But as Earl Long used to say about voting machines, there are ways to make scientific methodology play "Home, Sweet Home."

It's all in how the good doctors frame their inquiry. Like privately-commissioned political pollsters who produce desired results by asking artful questions, there are professors who know how to walk the line between the gods of science and the angels bestowing research funds.

Of course, whenever a grant is commissioned by an industry, the academic recipients make it absolutely clear that their integrity, the purity of their scientific method, won't be tainted by lucre. The study, they inform their patrons, will be free and independent—with no interference.

Certainly, the industrial donors respond. We wouldn't

120

have it any other way. Here's the lucre. Just go into your laboratories and let the chips fall where they may.

And they do, believe me, they do.

Now, if you buy that, let me tell you the one about how the stork brings cancer.

7.   Superdome:
The Great American Jock Itch

We people in New Orleans are sitting on some of the greatest assets in the world.

Former Mayor of New Orleans, Victor Hugo Schiro

———————◆———————

A Superdome in Central Park built during the administration of Mayor Mario Procaccino. Why not?

Too bad, really, that Mario Proccacino didn't have a Superdome fiction going for him or he would have defeated John Lindsay in the 1969 race for Mayor of New York. You remember Mario. He's Vic Schiro's Yankee soul brother-in-malaprop: the candidate who once reassured a friendly Democratic audience that though his running mate, Abe Beame, didn't make much of a first impression, "he grows on you, like a cancer."

Mario Procaccino, meet Vic Schiro. Vic, Mario.

What Mario needed as an adviser the year he lost to Lindsay was either Vic or Vic's campaign PR counsel, who happened to be my own asociate, Dave Kleck.

Kleck and I attended Tulane together in the years immediately after the Second World War. We later established a Washington-New Orleans PR agency affiliation, a fairly common practice between independent PR firms in different parts of the country. Dave needed a Washington outlet. I needed a legitimate reason to fly south three or four times a year for breakfast at Brennan's (one of his New Orleans clients). It was a business marriage made, if not in heaven, at IRS.

What would Kleck have advised Mario in the autumn of 1969? The same thing he advised Vic Schiro in 1965: "paint the big picture," and damn the cost.

"Fiction," says Kleck, outlining his theory of successful PR campaign management, "doesn't cost anything."

Well, that exaggerates even the big picture. For as these words are written, the going rate for steel and concrete fiction in New Orleans is $163,313,315, and rising. What the Superdome's going to cost by the time it's finished and ready for occupancy as the world's greatest sports-convention palace, nobody—not even with the structure 95 percent complete—is willing to guess.

But it's there, by God, a campaign fiction come to life. The biggest PR put-on in history, east or west of the Hudson. Why not? It got Vic Schiro re-elected Mayor of New Orleans, didn't it? And it put Kleck back in the good graces of an entrepreneur client, Dave Dixon, who had spent his adult life promoting our great American love affair with jockstraps.

If Marx were alive, you see, he would have to find a new axiom to grind: *sports-spectating* is the opiate of the people. A PR man who can lay hands on a sports vehicle to take-a-ride can do his client a service. Better still, let him lay hold of a sports vehicle for a client and do himself a service.

Kleck's done both. He handled the PR campaign that brought the Saints—then believed to be a professional football franchise—to New Orleans. He moved in during the final weeks of the 1965 mayoralty race to save Vic Schiro's political assets by painting "the big picture" of a Superdome over the city's horizon. And then, when campaign fiction became political reality, Kleck was there to sell Louisiana voters on a bond issue to build the dome.

But first, before the story of Schiro, the Saints, and the Superdome, a little pre-game background music involving Mario, the Mets, and Manhattan. And, oh yes, Marchi. My mayoral candidate, John Marchi, the thinking New Yorker's alternative to both Mario and the Great Profile.

1969: the year the Mets won the Series. This proved to be the most significant political occurrence of what, to that point, was a contest among three candidates—none of whom seemed to be able to get a grip on New York's disenchanted electorate.

There was Lindsay, the incumbent, a sure loser according to every media account I had read and heard. The Profile was running for re-election on the Liberal party line against Procaccino, Democrat, and Marchi, Republican-Conservative. Three losers in search of a handle.

Which was why I was on my way to the Biltmore Hotel to meet with Marchi on the day the Mets won the Series. The Conservative party of New York had retained me to contrive some way their candidate might overcome his Nice-Guy-But-Can't-win image. Despite his having defeated Lindsay in the Republican mayoral primary earlier that year, Marchi's campaign was sagging.

Conservatives, I love 'em. They're all cool logic. No emotional hang-ups such as the one clouding the thinking of the PR expert driving me to the Biltmore. You've met

124

the guy, I'm sure, if you've ever traveled commercially from LaGuardia. He's a member of the largest mobile political PR agency in the world: the New York Cab Drivers Association.

"Shit!" he began, slapping the meter hammer as the last out was retired in the Mets' upset win over the Baltimore Orioles.

"You have money on Baltimore?" I asked. No, he didn't. As a matter of fact, he was a Mets fan. But one who obviously had mixed emotions. Snapping off the post-game summary, he explained.

"It's just that, now we got to put up wit' *Lindsay* four more years. Mario is dead."

The first thing I did after arriving at John Marchi's hotel suite was try to loosen up Mr. Nice Guy with that story.

Now John Marchi, though he photographs like Pius XI reading the riot act on contraception, is a politician with a cool sense of humor. But he's also a man who thinks deep, introspective thoughts—a terrible handicap for a would-be leader called on to draw big pictures and disseminate vote-getting fictions in the final weeks of a political campaign.

"Unfortunately," said the thinking man's candidate, pondering the matter over a Campari on the rocks, "your taxicab expert is probably correct. Not that it's logical or reasonable. But any diversion from the city's problems tends to help the incumbent."

As if cool wit and introspection weren't bad enough, Marchi talked like that naturally. When he wasn't quoting Latin.

"You mean, the Mets win the Series, and *that* elects Lindsay?" I asked.

"Let me put it this way," Marchi said with a smile.

"Publicly, I'm delighted *our* Mets won. But, privately, I'd have picked another season."

For the next ten days, New York City was a Mets-crazed Roman circus. White and black, WASP and Puerto Rican, East Side-West Side, Staten Islander and Manhattanite, mugger and muggee—all joined hands.

Minor differences among races, creeds, occupations —along with police corruption, inadequate garbage collection, and anything John Marchi or Mario Procaccino had to say touching on municipal problems—were forgotten in the celebration of the city's greatest triumph since Grover Whalen was clipping ribbons. And John Lindsay, his title as incumbent mayor providing the crowbar, wedged himself into every public television and photo opportunity connected with the frenzy.

No post-election surveys were taken to measure the impact of the Mets' Series victory on Lindsay's successful re-election campaign. But for all of Mario Procaccino's verbal vagaries and John Marchi's intellectuality, the incumbent's victory margin wasn't much. Lindsay, in fact, won by a plurality, not a majority, with Mario running second and Mr. Nice Guy finishing where Nice Guys are supposed to finish—with or without PR help.

Looking back, I realize that my hack driver and candidate were absolutely right: in the final weeks of October, 1969, Tom Seaver was the best campaign manager John Lindsay had going for him.

So much for the way America's most sophisticated electorate faces up to its municipal problems. In the Deep South, suffering from more than a century of cultural-economic retardation, the escapism that afflicted New York City for three weeks in 1969 is a permanent condition, passed from generation to generation.

Jock-watching, especially *football* jock-watching, is at the heart of the Deep Southern life-style, running a close third in importance behind sexual intercourse between consenting (where possible) adults and bourbon-drinking. One way or another, all three figure into the political equation.

New Orleans in the mid-1960s was a community like all American communities. One plagued with racial tension, crime, and inadequate municipal services. But out of travail come men of vision and courage to lead the modern American urban dweller toward new vistas where rumbles, muggings, and the Full Garbage Pail are forgotten.

John Lindsay had Tom Seaver and the Mets. Vic Schiro, whether he appreciated them or not, had the two Daves—Dixon, the sports entrepreneur, and Kleck, the PR man who liked painting big pictures.

Dixon-Kleck's initial strategy to help New Orleanians forget their civic problems, while it seemed big at the time, was small fiction compared to the Superdome caper.

Dixon wanted to see his home town receive its proper recognition as one of the great cities of the Western World. The only man empowered to confer that distinction, by neo-Marxist axiom, was Pete Rozelle, Commissioner of the National Football League.

In 1962, Dixon retained Kleck to help bring a pro football franchise to town. Since pro football franchises are much-coveted by other communities with the jock itch, Kleck's PR assignment turned into a four-year account.

The original idea was to fill Tulane Stadium to 75,000-plus capacity for a couple of NFL pre-season games, then sit back and wait for the league to come running. But Pete Rozelle and the club owners of the

National Football League like to play pick-and-choose in handing out Great City awards. Dixon-Kleck filled the stadium twice, but received no phone calls. Rozelle, in fact, let it be known that Seattle and Tampa were ahead of New Orleans in the competition for an NFL franchise.

Then a funny thing happened to pro football on its way to the bank. A detour up to Capitol Hill. In order to complete the merger between the competing National and American Football Leagues, Rozelle needed special congressional legislation to exempt the "game" from general anti-trust laws governing other businesses.

The NFL-AFL merger bill went into the legislative hopper. It was expected to move quickly through both Houses of Congress. After all, what Senator or Congressman looking for 50-yard-line season tickets to see his home team play would block such a merger?

Only a few, but a very important few. One was Emanuel Celler. He was Chairman of the House Judiciary Committee and—bad news for pro football—an unregenerate Brooklyn Dodgers fan.

But the Brooklyn Dodgers, some young high school civics student is saying along about now, was a baseball team that relocated in Los Angeles in the late 1950s. What possible bearing could that have on whether pro *football* was permitted to merge in the mid-sixties?

Just this: old Manny Celler had never forgiven baseball for letting his favorite childhood team abandon Ebbets Field. And since it wasn't likely that professional baseball would ever pass through his committee in need of legislation, the chairman settled for the next best thing. Celler could hardly wait for the pro football merger bill to be assigned to his committee so that he could bottle it up.

So tell me, how do you teach this sort of thing to high school civics kids?

Enter now two of Dave Kleck's friends, Louisiana Senator Russell Long and New Orleans Congressman Hale Boggs. Long was a powerful member of the Senate Club. A merger bill would need his support to get through that body. Boggs was Majority Leader of the House. Kleck handled his PR during political campaigns. If anybody knew how to move a piece of legislation through or around old Manny Celler, it was Hale Boggs. And he could do just that—if the NFL would listen to reason about that New Orleans franchise.

What occurred between the two Louisianans and Pete Rozelle was a new form of legislative trade-off. Not pork-barreling: jock-barreling. You've got one of two choices, Long and Boggs told Rozelle and the leagues. You can give New Orleans a franchise and we'll take care of Manny Celler's roadblock. Or you can go to Los Angeles and talk Walter O'Malley into bringing the Dodgers back to Brooklyn.

Rozelle, who began his career as a sports PR flack, got the big picture. On All Saints Day, the same year— nice PR datesmanship—the NFL Commissioner announced that the National Conference of a newly merged professional football league would field a team from New Orleans. The Saints came marchin' in.

And that, class, is how a pro franchise is born.

Meanwhile, back in New Orleans, Dave Dixon had somewhere along the way wearied of having just a single speculative ball in the air. Even as Rozelle was playing hard to get, Dixon was looking beyond what he considered the inevitable day when New Orleans would field a professional football team.

Despite the presence of the Saints, some would say that day is yet to arrive. The stadium, though derisively referred to by some as "the last great monument to American folly," nevertheless—in the words of *The New York*

Times—"now stands in downtown New Orleans like a Montana mountain."

In the beginning, ten years ago, the new stadium wasn't supposed to be standing *downtown*, but somewhere on a "mystery tract" in eastern New Orleans. That was in the days when the Superdome was still just another one of Dave Dixon's harebrained promotional schemes, however. He was its sole supporter, in fact. Things might have stayed that way, too, except for Vic Schiro's 1965 re-election problems. The Great Profile had the Mets to distract his jock-minded constituents. But Vic, without Tom Seaver around, needed something else.

What he got was Dave Kleck and the big picture. Kleck was called in to be "of counsel" during the closing weeks of the 1965 New Orleans mayoralty race, in the same way I was brought in to try to salvage John Marchi's campaign. But happily for his New Orleans candidate, my associate possessed the visceral PR wisdom of both my Manhattan cab driver and candidate.

Which brings us, class, finally, to the subject of how a Superdome is born.

When Kleck came to the New Orleans mayoralty campaign, Schiro was trailing his opponent, Jimmy Fitzmorris (since elected Lieutenant Governor), in a tight race. What's more, with only a few weeks left, all the campaign momentum seemed to be in Fitzmorris' favor. Kleck proposed an immediate change in strategy. He presented it to Schiro's campaign manager, Salvador Anzelmo, a member of the New Orleans delegation to the State Legislature.

Up to that point, the incumbent mayor had spent his time in public appearances and on television trying to defend his administration's four-year record from Fitzmorris' attacks. This strategy, the PR counsel told Anzelmo, was playing the opponent's game.

You don't get voters' minds off race riots, crime, and poor garbage collection by defending your record on race riots, crime, and poor garbage collection, Kleck argued. Schiro has to change the subject.

Lift their eyes from the overflowing pail to the blue horizon. Paint a glowing future, not simply for the voters of 1965, but for their children and their children's children.

Get to the point, said Anzelmo.

Talk in terms of a single, dramatic, mind-boggling civic project, continued Kleck. A project at once *abstract* and *visible.*

What did Kleck have in mind, specifically?

Well, it so happened that the PR counsel had this other client, Dave Dixon. You know, Dixon, the pro football franchise zealot? Now Dixon has this other project. He calls it "the Superdome." If Schiro embraced the idea of building a Superdome, then Dixon would help him paint the picture. He would go on the boob tube with Vic and tell the voters how Schiro was going to put New Orleans on the map.

Schiro's campaign manager listened. But it was clear to Kleck that he wasn't convinced that kind of smoke could turn a political race around.

Anzelmo was a nuts-and-bolts politician. He wanted details. For example: where would the land come from? A Superdome, it's gotta be located on *land* somewhere, right?

Kleck had just the man there, too. A new developer in the community, Marvin Kratter. A would-be political kingmaker. The kind of operator who flies Hubert Humphrey around in his private plane. Kratter had a mammoth tract of land in eastern New Orleans. Would Marvin donate two hundred acres to build a Superdome? Of course Marvin would. Would he do it on television with the mayor? Is the Pope ecumenical? Sure he would. Try to keep him off.

O.K., nodded Anzelmo, you've got some land. But what about the financing? The city was taxed to the limit, practically penniless. The North Louisiana redneck legislators wouldn't vote funds for a Superdome in wicked New Orleans, even if they believed you were actually going to *build* one with the funds they voted. So how could it be financed?

Simple, said Kleck. Lie. Not a criminal or venal lie, but just an innocent lie, in the grandest of all Louisiana traditions. A political lie. We'll say it will be half-public, half-private financing. The mayor has it all figured out, but he's not going to tell anyone until after the election.

Anzelmo nodded, but he was still obviously troubled. Kleck was talking about an *idea*. But not anything people could see or put their finger on. No problem, said Kleck. When the mayor gets on television to talk about the Superdome, he'll have drawings. Kleck's agency artist always wanted to design a domed stadium. Now he would. All kinds of designs and drawings.

Inside. Outside. The fantastic, giant, instant-replay screen, etc.

Anzelmo was sold; they would go with the Super-dome idea. Kleck was on the verge of pulling off one of the great political PR ploys of the decade when suddenly, natural forces intervened, in two disparate forms.

First, Betsy, one of the worst hurricanes in the city's history, hit New Orleans. It was no time for Superdome talk. Vic Schiro was in the streets visiting severe damage areas, while his opponent was on television implying that on top of riots, crime, and bad garbage collection, the incumbent was now in a vile conspiracy with the elements.

Stung, Schiro lashed back in his best Procaccino-vian form. On the radio at midnight he warned the people against Fitzmorris' exaggeration of actual damage to the city. "Do not believe any of those false rumors," the mayor cautioned his listeners, "unless you hear them from me."

"Do you know what you just said in there?" a newsman asked the mayor as he left the studio. Apprised of his blooper, Schiro shrugged, "Well," he said wearily, "that's the way the cookie bounces."

Finally, responsibility for the hurricane died out as a central issue in the mayoralty campaign. Kleck was called by Anzelmo and told that Vic "is set to go with the dome idea."

Almost, but not quite. At the last minute, as Kleck was putting finishing touches on his script, Vic Schiro suffered an appendicitis attack and was rushed to the hospital for an emergency operation. With only a week left and the candidate out of action, what do you do? Go with the next best thing.

Kleck wrote a television tearjerker for Mrs. Schiro. Nothing about the Superdome, of course. Just good, basic, appeal-to-reason stuff.

"I speak to you now (pause)," said Mrs. Sunny Schiro into Camera No. 1, "for the man you call (pause, catch in throat) the Little Guy in City Hall . . ."

It went over so well that Jimmy Fitzmorris started spreading word that the Little Guy in City Hall had faked his operation.

Coming down to the final days of the campaign, the surveys showed Schiro on the move. But not fast enough to catch up with Fitzmorris' lead before election day. Then seventy-two hours before the polls were to open, Anzelmo called Kleck to report good news: "We are going with the Superdome," he said. "But Vic can't be moved to a TV studio. The show will have to be done at his home. Sorry."

"Sorry?" Kleck exulted. "Make it in his *bathrobe*, you understand? Be sure he's in his bathrobe!"

Anzelmo didn't understand. "You want the *scars* showing?" he said. No, the PR man replied, no scars—just the robe. And one more thing; word about the Superdome announcement wasn't to get out of the campaign inner circle. Fitzmorris had to be taken by surprise so that he couldn't sink the idea before it floated.

To make sure of this, Kleck placed a devious newspaper ad, run the day before election, promoting Schiro's final televised vote appeal as "A Fireside Chat with Sunny and Vic."

On the evening the Superdome was born, Kleck, Dixon, and Kratter, the land developer, showed up at the mayor's residence hours early to rehearse the show. The PR counsel turned the script over to Schiro and began briefing His Excellency. For all the weeks of talk about "the bombshell," this was actually Kleck's first chance to review the plan with the candidate.

Vic Schiro, for all his malapropensity, was a consummate political animal. It took him ten minutes to review the entire thirty-minute TV script, including his address. When the mayor finished, he laid it aside and leaned over to shake Kleck's hand:

"This," he smiled, "is the election. Only one thing bothers me, though."

(Thirty minutes to airtime.)

"What?" Kleck asked nervously.

"Explain again," said Schiro. "*How* did I finance it?"

Kleck reviewed the specious nature of the financing. The candidate assured him that he had matters under control.

But now something bothered the PR counsel. The phones would be ringing off the hook as soon as the show was over, he told the mayor. Some newsman was bound to ask why the mayor had waited until just before election to announce detailed plans for "the greatest domed stadium in the history of the world."

"Hell, don't worry about that one," replied Vic Shiro, straightening his kimono and getting ready for the cameras. "I'll just say, *Can you think of a better time?*"

Dave Kleck was at home late election eve, savoring a self-congratulatory drink, when the telephone rang. It was his old friend, Jimmy Fitzmorris, the opponent who, like Vic Schiro, instantly recognized the significance of what he had witnessed on the tube a few hours earlier. It was one of those sublime moments of political *angst*, Kleck recalls.

"Dave," said the future Lieutenant Governor of Louisiana, "there are some things in this rotten business that just aren't *fair*, you know? They say they're gonna have a 'Fireside Chat with Sunny and Vic,' right? So I turn on my set and what do I get? A fuckin' Superdome!"

HISTORICAL NOTE (1)

Vic Schiro was re-elected Mayor of New Orleans in 1965 by 435 votes out of more than 200,000 cast.

HISTORICAL NOTE (2)

In Baton Rouge, ninety miles north of New Orleans, Governor John McKeithen studied the returns with the eye of a professional who grasped Big Pictures like fistfuls of salted peanuts. McKeithen told a friend that the Superdome idea had swung 10,000 votes to the winning side.

135

The Governor, geared for a re-election campaign himself, began pushing for a constitutional amendment to permit the floating of state-backed bonds for construction of the "Greatest Domed Stadium in the World."

Kleck was called in. With only a $60,000 PR advertising budget, he helped the Governor win 85 percent voter approval in a statewide referendum to create a Superdome Authority. The campaign fiction was now a political reality. But there were still obstacles that had to be overcome before the Superdome could take on a life of its own beyond the will or whim of even the people who helped create it.

Five years later, McKeithen, having won re-election, came up against one such obstacle:

The redneck Louisiana legislature, never really happy with the idea, was threatening to put the Superdome Authority out of business. The Governor asked Dave Dixon, now executive director of the Authority, to make a statewide television address on the eve of the legislative session. Kleck was again brought in, to draft the speech.

The PR man holed up with Dixon and began pounding away on a thirty-minute stem-winder, choosing as his theme "Small-Minded Men Through History." It was an assault on all those myopic pygmies who, over the centuries, argued against giant strides in human progress, e.g., Columbus' voyages, Fulton's steamboat, the Golden Gate Bridge, the Cow Palace, etc.

Dixon, peering over his speechwriter's shoulder had a suggestion.

"Don't forget," he said, "the jerks up in Manhattan who warned that if Al Smith ever went through with the Empire State Building it would cause unceasing rain."

Kleck, who hadn't previously heard of that incident, inserted the line. Dixon video-taped the speech. Later that night the two were watching their collaborative pitch to the people of Louisiana. It was an appeal for jock-lovers and believers in human progress to write, wire, and call their representatives in Baton Rouge to support the Superdome Authority.

Dixon-on-the-tube, video-taped, was saying: ". . . and then there were those small-minded men who claimed that if they built that great structure, the Empire State Building, it would cause unceasing rain . . ."

Dixon-in-the-flesh, sitting next to Kleck, looked uneasy.

"What's wrong with that?" asked the PR man. 'It's a great line."

"Yeah," said Dixon, "but I hope it's not misleading, you know? I mean, *somebody* in New York must've said something like that. Don't you think?"

HISTORICAL NOTE (3)

Excerpts from The New York Times, *February 3, 1974:*

" . . . When the dome was proposed in 1965, a year before the state's voters approved it, it was supposed to cost between $20 and $30 million . . .

"Mr. Levy, who did not join the dome staff until 1972, is in the unhappy position of having to explain why his predecessors in the project misled the public on the cost . . .

"A committee of the state legislature is trying to find out why the costs have gone so high. The investigation was begun after the dome commission asked the state last fall to approve an additional $8 million to finish construction . . ."

HISTORICAL NOTE (4)

GREAT THOUGHTS OF SOUTHERN MAN
"Explain again. *How* did I finance it?"

8.   Hollywood West, Hollywood East

Bogie fought the press when he was young, but in later years he mellowed. "Get along with 'em," he'd tell me. "You can't win." I tried that for a while. It didn't work. So I say, screw 'em.

> Theory of PR, Francis Albert Sinatra to author, June, 1972

———◆———

Every five years, give or take a congressional session, some new Senate or House committee tries to recapture the headline glory of Estes Kefauver's original crime investigators. This makes for two to four weeks of hot rehashed Mafioso stories, after which everybody—the country, the Congress, the Cosa Nostra—returns to normal.

Kefauver's original script, with Frank Costello playing the lead witness, was high Capitol Hill melodrama in 1951. Successive congressional crime investigations have been dull by comparison. Like *Planet of the Apes* sequels, they're only low-budget imitations.

In spring, 1972, however, Congressman Claude Pepper's Select House Committee on Crime had a little something extra going for it: *The Godfather*. Both the book and the motion picture were breaking sales records, inspiring a new Mafia fan cult.

Pepper's committee was looking into criminal influence on horse racing in the Northeast one day, questioning a character named Joe (The Baron) Barboza. The witness was a convicted triggerman for the New England mob, serving a life sentence for murder. Suddenly, to the delight of a drowsy press, he dropped Frank Sinatra's name into the proceedings.

Jackpot for the Pepper comittee: WITNESS LINKS SINATRA WITH REPUTED MAFIA FIGURE, screeched the afternoon headlines.

Not long after, Sinatra came to Washington with his lawyer, Mickey Rudin, to refute testimony by Barboza that the singer was an intimate of Raymond Patriarca, the Godfather of New England. The story behind the headline was that Sinatra had bought 5 percent of a Massachusetts racetrack in which Patriarca owned shares. Unknown to Sinatra, his name was listed as a member of the track board of directors.

It was the old familiar congressional committee publicity game. First, Sinatra didn't know Patriarca. Next, Barboza's testimony—hearsay from a witness who had already confessed to twenty-seven gangland executions—was less than unimpeachable. The national office of the American Civil Liberties Union, in fact, registered a strong protest with Pepper for letting the Barboza statement go into the record unchallenged.

But the Select House Committee on Crime wasn't looking any gift headlines in the mouth. Up to the moment Barboza testified, the hearings had been droning along; the name Sinatra put their investigation on the front page.

The PR man's insatiable urge to kibitz with the fortune and reputation of others—particularly upper-case Others—led me to Sinatra's suite at the Madison Hotel on the afternoon before he was scheduled to testify. My idea was to give him a few hours of gratuitous advice on how to handle his dilemma. Tune him in to the vibes of political PR in the Nation's Capital.

One big problem there, however, was that Sinatra, whom I came to know because of his friendship with Spiro Agnew, didn't figure *he* was the party with the dilemma. The way the singer sized up the situation, it was the *committee* that was in trouble. Still, he was a cordial host, nodding attentively while I offered choice counsel drawn from a dozen years' experience dealing with congressional committees on behalf of clients.

My proposal was that Sinatra consider the Pepper hearing itself a no-win proposition. I told him that a witness who testifies before a congressional committee is playing on the other fellow's publicity turf. My advice was that he go before the committee next day, take his lumps, then hold a news conference afterward. Answer all questions in a format that he, not the committee, controlled. Make copies of all pertinent documents available to the press (Rudin had a stack of legal documents disproving any Sinatra link with Patriarca).

"Upstage Pepper's act with your own," I advised. "Then after the news conference invite one or two friendly reporters up to your suite for a drink. I know a couple who'd cut their throats for an interview with Frank Sinatra."

"Or mine if they get one," Sinatra replied. He had heard me out, patiently. All good advice, he conceded. Except for one basic flaw.

"I've got it figured differently," he informed me. "My idea is to *fight*, not kiss anybody's ass."

"*Fight* a congressional committee?" I said. "Nobody's gotten away with that since Howard Hughes."

Judging from Sinatra's expression on hearing that piece of Washington history, I got the feeling that if there *had* been any doubt in his mind about what he intended to do, I'd just resolved it.

The Pepper committee convened in Room 345 of the Cannon Office Building at eleven o'clock the next morning. By 11:30, Howard Hughes had to move over.

The committee had given a publicity platform, Sinatra told Pepper and his colleagues, to a "bum running off at the mouth."

"It was a character assassination, let's face it," Sinatra declared, to the periodic *ooh's, aah's,* and applause of an audience of congressional secretaries that filled the committee room. "I resent it. I won't have it. I am *not* a second-class citizen. *Let's get that straightened out.*"

Straightened out it was. As the conclusion of Sinatra's testimony, Congressman John Murphy of New York told the witness that he felt the committee had been "taken advantage of" by Barboza.

"I don't know you," Murphy told Sinatra, "I have never met you. I just know you by what I read in the paper and your reputation as an entertainer. But I would like to explain to the people in the audience today, and I know my colleagues on the committee share the feeling, that we are taken advantage of in certain situations and I, as one member of the committee, resent it and appreciate your appearing here today."

On the way out of the Cannon Office Building, Sinatra blew by the waiting Washington press corps— just the way I'd advised him not to. He headed for National Airport, boarded his private plane, and was comfortably settled into his Palm Springs villa by the time the evening news was reporting his PR coup. Never, wrote Mary McGrory in a follow-up column in the *Evening Star-*

141

News next day, had she witnessed so many obsequious Congressmen stumbling over each other's feet in one committee room.

So much for tuning Frank Sinatra in to the vibes of political PR in the Nation's Capital.

Actually, Frank Sinatra's PR problems held more than a kibitzing fascination for Spiro Agnew's press secretary. Every story coming out of the Pepper hearings included some reference to the singer's friendship with the Vice President. Incoming mail told me that Sinatra's PR, good or bad, had a subsequent fall-out effect on my client.

I once asked my secretary, Lisa Brown, to do a letter survey on news-and-column coverage of the Agnew-Sinatra relationship. She estimated that over a three-month period, one item by "Walter Scott" in *Parade* magazine was worth fifty hate-o-grams from around the country. A gossip column mention by Maxine Cheshire brought in ten to twenty.

Not much. But nothing to slough off, either, since most of the letters came from Agnew's Middle American constituency. Church-going salt o' the earth people who would have preferred to read about their hero teeing up with Pat Boone.

Agnew, however, blamed this constituent backlash on "the damned news media."

"The day I let *The Washington Post* pick my friends is the day I get out of politics," he once told me. In that sentiment he touched on one of the strongest bonds between himself and Sinatra: an abiding contempt for the national press.

The Agnew-Sinatra friendship had come about through Pete Malatesta, the Vice President's political aide on the road. A nephew of Bob Hope and a onetime Los

Angeles PR man, Malatesta joined Agnew a few months after I did. He was my closest friend and associate on the staff. We worked together as a road team; I handled press, while Pete took care of the pols and celebrities.

Malatesta's PR gift was an ability to put the right people together at the right time. Better, it was *knowing* the right people to put together at the right time. He knew Sinatra from his early Los Angeles days and waited for the chance to introduce the singer and his new employer.

The right time came one afternoon in early 1971, when we were at the Canyon Hotel in Palm Springs, Agnew's favorite spa. Pete asked the Veep if he had a golf partner for the next day. Agnew didn't. Next thing, Malatesta was on the phone asking Sinatra if he'd like to play golf the following morning with the Vice President of the United States.

It was an offer Sinatra couldn't refuse.

Malatesta's serendipitist instincts never served an employer better. Sinatra, the second-generation Italian-American who did it his way, and Agnew, the second-generation Greek-American who did it his way, were in full sync by the time their golf cart reached the second tee.

Sinatra had supported liberal Democratic candidates all his life. He'd been used, then cast off by the Kennedys (he had liked Jack, despised Bobby, and spoke only with contempt about Teddy). In 1968, he went down the line for his friend, Hubert Humphrey.

Less than a year before meeting Agnew, however, the singer had begun a political matamorphosis, endorsing the re-election candidacy of Governor Ronald Reagan. The Agnew association helped the conversion along. But some of Sinatra's old liberal friends were shaken when word first circulated about his new VIP guest at Palm Springs.

"What could Frank Sinatra and Spiro Agnew possibly have in common?" sniffed Democrat activist Shirley Mac-Laine. "I mean, what do they *talk* about when they're together?"

The question was relayed to Sinatra. He sent word back: "Tell Shirley, 'we talk about *you*, baby.'"

In fact, they talked about politics, music, sports—and, of course, their shared abhorrence of the news media. But beyond these interests something more adhesive cemented the Agnew-Sinatra friendship. Each man, in his own way, was starstruck. One by Celebrity, the other by Power.

Pete Malatesta, a PR man with a foot in both worlds, recognized the mutual attraction of politicians and show biz stars in a formula he worked out for successful party-giving.

"The right mix for a party in Malibu is a roomful of stars and one politician flown in from Washington," Pete once told me. "For a party in Georgetown, a roomful of politicians and one star flown in from Hollywood."

This cross-pollination of Celebrity and Power was presaged by Franklin Roosevelt's use of show business endorsements in his re-election campaigns during the war years. But the process didn't reach full bloom until the advent of (1) the coaxial cable, and (2) the Kennedys.

The cable brought national network news into the American living room every sundown. The once-faceless functionaries who run our Government suddenly had faces. And with faces, Celebrity. By the early 1970s, a Secretary of State who wouldn't have been recognized anywhere but Harvard Square a few years before could become the toast of Hollywood West, a household accent in Peoria.

John F. Kennedy's brief tenure in the White House merged Celebrity and Power into the great American PR dream. More than anything else, it was Kennedy and the legend of his Presidency that transformed the Nation's Capital—once a dull city of bureaucrats and stuffed shirts —into Hollywood East.

Before the days of Camelot, the height of the political social season in the Nation's Capital was the annual Gridiron Club dinner. Being invited to that white-tie affair, sponsored by the exclusive Washington correspondents' club, was mandatory for any public relations body-who-was-anybody. Celebrities from around the world were on hand, and to wheedle an invitation for a client was status in the bank.

Nevertheless, Spiro Agnew's only head-to-head battle with Richard Nixon involved the Vice President's unwillingness to attend the Gridiron dinner of 1971.

In the first spring of the Nixon-Agnew Administration, the two men did a piano duet at a Gridiron affair. The following year, Nixon attended as guest of honor. But the President wanted Agnew to fill in for him in 1971. Agnew, as befits an heir-apparent to the American Presidency, always did what the White House wanted him to do. But when the request came in from Herb Klein, Nixon's communications director, to attend the '71 Gridiron, the Vice President drew the line.

His position was that he'd been to one Gridiron. And if you've been to one . . .

The struggle raged for four months, with me, the Vice President's press secretary, in the middle. After

Klein, higher-ranking White House aides began pushing the request, but Agnew wouldn't budge.

"If the President wants me to go," he said, "let him ask me himself."

Two weeks before the dinner, word came from Bob Haldeman, the man next to Nixon, that the President would appreciate Agnew's attending in his place. Incredibly, Agnew still said no. Until, one week prior to the event, Nixon sent direct word. Or was it direct word? He didn't call Agnew, which would have taken all of thirty seconds. Instead, the President of the United States wrote to the Vice President—in longhand—asking that Agnew do the Old Man this one favor.

The letter did the job; Agnew relented. He attended the dinner and with the help of Ray Siller's gag material even got an enthusiastic response from his Eastern liberal press audience. But it was Agnew's last Gridiron. The following year Nixon took the cowardly, easy way: he went himself.

For fifty years the Gridiron was the Only-Place-to-Be in Washington on a given night in spring. But in Hollywood East, post-Kennedy, there are other places where PR men and their clients can gather with members of the news media and bask in an aura of Celebrity and Power.

The Sans Souci Restaurant, across Pennsylvania Avenue from the White House, is where Hollywood East often meets Hollywood West at midday, Monday through Friday. Kissinger can be seen lunching with Tinseltown gossip columnist Joyce Haber or Norman Mailer. Art Buchwald, at the same table every day, shares political bons mots with Ethel Kennedy, Edward Bennett Williams, and George Stevens, Jr. And every so often, when he's in town, Charlton Heston drops by. Or Robert Redford. Or Eva Gabor.

A few blocks north on Connecticut Avenue is Paul Young's, where Joseph Kennedy hosted a lavish January, 1961, pre-Inaugural party ushering in the Kennedy era, and where the big-spending lapel-strokers meet Capitol Hill friends for dinner.

Power feeds off Celebrity in Hollywood East, and the feeding is mutual. The game at the Sans Souci and Paul Young's is See-and-Be-Seen:

Rowlie Evans is lunching with a senior White House aide (watch his column in the next few days to find out what one faction around the President is saying about another). There's Pete Malatesta with Freddie Brisson, Roz Russell's husband. (Drop by the table on the way out. It never hurts for people to know-who-you-know . . .)

In Hollywood East, there are also more kinetic media lights to turn on than those found at stuffy Gridirons.

The Valkyries, for example, can make or break a political image faster than Scotty Reston or Joe Kraft. And not one belongs to the Gridiron Club, because until recently it excluded women: there's Sally Quinn of *The Washington Post*; Kandy Stroud, formerly of *Women's Wear Daily*; Betty Beale, the syndicated columnist.

Some of the most potent journalism coming out of Washington in recent years has been the product of news-women/persons covering the Power and Celebrity circuit.

The politician or his PR man who gets distracted by blonde hair and a radiant smile—mistaking a Quinn or Stroud for a traditional "society-page reporter"—will come away from an interview with severe contusions. Both are tough-minded political writers.

Kandy Stroud had a shipwreck impact on the Muskie

Presidential campaign. She was the interviewer who did the feature piece on Mrs. Muskie—reprinted by *Newsweek* and then by William Loeb's *Manchester Union-Leader*—that led to the Senator's flatbed truck crying jag in the New Hampshire snow. The incident is generally regarded as the downward turning point in the Muskie Presidential campaign of 1972.

Sally Quinn, after a six-month fling at CBS, returned to her *Washington Post* beat in mid-1974. One of her first major features was on Steve Martindale, a young account executive for Hill & Knowlton's Washington office.

Although PR operators ought to know better than to reveal their *modus operandi*, Martindale submitted to the Quinn treatment. The result was a penetrating study of one technique of PR lapel-stroking.

Quinn detailed the Martindale method of putting together Washington Celebrity-Power social events: How he cultivated the friendship of Joan Braden, wife of syndicated columnist Tom Braden, by throwing a birthday party for her, and then used her name as a lure to attract Henry Kissinger, Alice Roosevelt Longworth, and other prestigious guests (none of whom knew him personally) into his home. After which, the host parlayed the event into an entrée to other important contacts.

Quinn's story also outlined the PR subtleties of whiplashing big-name attendance at Hollywood East parties: first, you call Kissinger's office, informing his social secretary that Mrs. Longworth plans to be at the event. Hang up and reverse the process, call Mrs. Longworth to tell her Henry will be there. So far, so good. Now, if you can fly in a Hollywood West superstar as an added lure . . .

Franklin D. Roosevelt's PR aides lifted the idea of using celebrities in political campaigns from U.S. war bond drives. His campaign managers figured that if show biz stars could persuade people to buy bonds in the national interest, the same appeal could work in partisan politics.

They started something. At first, the big motion picture studios tried to keep their flesh-and-blood properties from involvement in politics. The traditional PR wisdom of the nineteen-forties was that an entertainer who took sides between two Presidential candidates would lose box office appeal among large segments of the public. But the lure of access to White House power dulled such fears. By the mid-forties, Celebrity-and-Artist committees were PR adjuncts of every national campaign.

The Democrats have always had an edge in these celebrity draws because most creative artists lean toward liberal causes. But the Republicans have had their tinsel cadres. From the early days, John Wayne headed a list that included Gloria Swanson, Lloyd Nolan, Robert Montgomery, Adolphe Menjou, and Ward Bond. More recently, newer television stars—Clint Walker, Efrem Zimbalist, Jr., Buddy Ebsen, among others—have helped Republican candidates.

By the 1960s, election year recruiting competition between the parties, not only for motion picture and TV stars but big name athletes, became fierce. The Kennedys put celebrity-gathering into mass production. Not even FDR in his wartime 1944 campaign enlisted as many show biz and sports stars as did JFK in 1960.

The two categories of stardom served different campaign purposes, however. Motion picture-TV entertainers are best for fund-raising at rallies and private fatcat functions. Athletes enhance the image of the candidate more directly: All-Americanism by association.

Celebrity and sports endorsements played a key PR role in the Kennedy-Nixon 1960 race. The impact of the

Kennedy campaign's successful star and jock recruitments made a deep impression on Nixon's PR outlook in later Presidential races.

In 1960, the Nixon image-strategy was to juxtapose his own maturity and experience in government alongside his opponent's youth. Kennedy, on the other hand, was stressing his youth through mass sports endorsements. In the end, Youth-and-Vigor edged Maturity-and-Experience. Nixon took the lesson to heart.

There's no PR student like a politician who's lost an election. In 1968, Nixon gave formation of his Celebrity-and-Sports committee high campaign priority.

Jan Rus, a Los Angeles businessman with wide contacts in both amateur and professional sports, was assigned the job of breaking John Kennedy's previous record in gathering sports endorsements. Rus, the man who introduced Nixon to Coach George Allen, entered into pitched battle with Hubert Humphrey's sports endorsement scouts.

Because of the increasing importance of the black vote, one of the most sought-after athletes was Gale Sayers of the Chicago Bears. Sayers' services in the '68 campaign were more actively sought than at any time since the superstud halfback graduated from high school. Sayers switched sides twice—due to misunderstandings, he said—but finally signed his letter of intent with Humphrey.

Rus, however, didn't lose many other jock supporters for his Presidential candidate. By the end of the campaign, Nixon boasted more than six hundred sports endorsements—the largest number in Presidential campaign history. Rus personally enlisted over four hundred "Athletes for Nixon-Agnew."

Out in Hollywood West, however, recruiting came harder. Even after he moved into the White House, Nixon attracted fewer show biz personalities to his side than any President since the Celebrity-Power cross-pollination process began.

Nixon had Bob Hope, Jackie Gleason, Pat Boone, Art Linkletter, and later, Sammy Davis, Jr. But he wanted more. While superficially disdaining the swinging Kennedy style—the Billy Graham Sunday prayer sessions in the East Room were Dick and Pat's Middle American answer to the avant-garde cultural ambience of Jack and Jackie's White House—Nixon had an itch for the Hollywood West adulation enjoyed by the Kennedys.

There's no other way to explain, for example, the ongoing hypocrisy of the Nixon White House regarding Spiro Agnew's friendship with Frank Sinatra.

Publicly, through calculated leaks to the press, White House staffmen tongue-clucked over the Agnew-Sinatra relationship. Every Sinatra controversy that hit print— notably, his $2-in-a-glass hassle with gossip columnist Maxine Cheshire—produced a spate of White House-inspired stories about Nixon's embarrassment over the fact that his Vice President kept bad company.

But while Ron Ziegler's staff was putting out this PR line over one phone, Bob Haldeman was on another extension asking Pete Malatesta whether he could arrange, without too much fanfare, a Nixon-Sinatra golf game during one of the President's frequent visits to the West Coast.

For a long time, Malatesta, who resented the official White House put-down of the Agnew-Sinatra connection, sat on Haldeman's request. But finally he did arrange a Nixon-Sinatra get-together on the golf links—only to get caught up in one of the biggest outdoor social snafus of the Nixon Administration.

We called it the Battle of the Super-egos. It occurred

because on this one occasion Malatesta over-achieved in bringing the right people together at the right time.

Challenge for a PR serendipitist: how do you fit one U.S. President, one U.S. Vice President, one Bob Hope, and one Frank Sinatra into two golf carts? It's not as simple as it might appear to an outsider unfamiliar with the problems posed by Super-egos in heat.

The correct answer? You bring in a fifth playing partner. Let me explain . . .

Agnew was visiting Sinatra at Palm Springs and Nixon was down the road at San Clemente. Through Paul Keyes, the *Laugh-In* producer-gagwriter, word was relayed to Malatesta that Nixon wanted to play a round of golf with (in order of Presidential preference): Sinatra, Hope, and his Vice President.

It was easy enough to put the match together. But although diplomatic protocol establishes seating arrangements at White House dinners, no similar rules exist for golf cart placement.

Since Agnew was Sinatra's Palm Springs houseguest, the golf cart pair-ups in seating should have been Nixon-Hope in Cart No. 1 and Agnew-Sinatra in Cart No. 2. But the President, as noted, was eager to bring Sinatra into his limited Hollywood celebrity circle. He sent word that arrangements be made for Nixon-Sinatra and Agnew-Hope pair-ups.

On the evening preceding the match, Hope got word that he would ride with Avis, not Hertz. It didn't sit well, not at all. Bob Hope takes a back cart to no living superstar, Hollywood East or West.

Because Malatesta had arranged for the game, Hope assumed his nephew had also handled its golf-cart seating. Pete got an avuncular blistering over the phone. But shrewdly—since it would only have made a bad situation worse—he took the heat and didn't inform Hope that it was the President's, not Agnew's staff, who had requested the Nixon-Sinatra cartpool.

When Malatesta hung up, his ears ringing with the imprecations of America's foremost funnyman, he foresaw trouble along the fairways. Going back to the President's staff to ask that Nixon reverse his historic cart-riding decision was out of the question, however. That would be interpreted as a request coming from the Vice President, leading to even worse protocol headaches. Avis, you see, doesn't second-guess Hertz on the Really Big Ones.

But for the sake of his own family amity, how could Malatesta get Nixon to give up his idea of riding with Sinatra? The only way, Pete concluded, was to pose a *real* problem in protocol when the group teed up.

Ronald Reagan was scheduled to fly to San Clemente to visit Nixon the next day. If the Governor of California could move his trip up a few hours . . .

Through a series of adroit long-distance moves, Malatesta arranged just that. With the Governor on the premises, it made for an awkward fivesome. But the Battle of the Super-egos was resolved—in a draw.

Nixon rode with Reagan.

Sinatra with Agnew.

And Hope with his nephew—who just went along for an earful of laughs.

9. Law and PR-der: Attorneys General I Have Known

Public opinion is the last refuge of a scoundrel.

Samuel Johnson (brother of Lyndon)

———◆———

Like criminal lawyers and psychiatrists, PR men earn their best money when a big client is in big trouble. Bad luck for the client: good fortune for his PR counsel.

Still, as a PR man, I had bad luck with my Attorneys General. Or was it the reverse?

The *first* law-and-order politician I ever met was Silas Comer Garrett, Attorney General of Alabama, 1951 to 1955. Good old happy-go-lucky Si. Not long after we were introduced and enjoyed a pleasant dinner together in downtown Birmingham, he was charged with vote fraud, indicted for conspiracy to murder, and whisked off to Sealy sanitarium, the Texas funny farm for Very Important Politicians (where a loving Long family tried, unsuccessfully, to commit Uncle Earl in his declining days).

I helped the *second* Attorney General I ever met get

elected. Remember Richmond Flowers? He was convicted of extortion in office and sent to a Federal penitentiary.

Given that experience with state Attorneys General, my obvious move was to step up a grade. I did when I got to know a U.S. Attorney General: John Mitchell.

To be fair to myself, Si Garrett had flipped long before we met. Nothing any other PR counsel might have done could have salvaged the man or his image. He was a case for a psychiatrist rather than a PR man, which is not really unusual for a politician, except when it becomes a matter of public knowledge.

But in the cases of Flowers, my second A-G acquaintance, and Mitchell, my third, I often find myself wondering whether something I did—or didn't do—might have made a difference in the way their careers ended. In Flowers' case, I agreed to help him during an election. In Mitchell's, I refused. Question: (1) if I hadn't helped Rich, maybe he would have *lost* that 1962 race and stayed out of prison; (2) if I had gone to work for Mitchell in early 1972 . . . but this gets ahead of the story. Before Mitchell, there was Flowers.

Understand, when I claim I helped elect Rich, it's only the occupational hyperbole of a PR man who's participated in a winning campaign. Had Flowers been defeated, I wouldn't claim credit for helping him blow the race. The standard professional line under those circumstances is, "If the candidate had only listened to my advice . . ." (For further amplification on this point, see Chapter 4, re Shirley Temple Black's campaign.)

Still, when Rich's advisers called me in from Washington, it looked like he might have a tough time pulling the race out. He had a 40,000-vote lead in the first Alabama primary—in those days, winning the Democratic

155

primary was equivalent to election. But it was a scary 40,000. According to the vote breakdown, Flowers carried all the black precincts in Birmingham, Montgomery, and Mobile: *bad news.*

What was bad news about winning those precincts had to do with regional political customs of the time. Flowers' opponent, Willard Livingston, had already zeroed in on those figures during the run-off race, appealing to the white majority to unify against the "Black bloc vote."

This was known as the "Black Hand" technique. A decade ago, before the Voting Rights Act, it constituted the most feared political propaganda weapon in Southern politics. Even with the Voting Rights Act, it's a technique that's worked at times in other, theoretically more "liberal" areas of the country.

In Los Angeles, for example, during the mayoralty race of 1970, Sam Yorty, then the incumbent mayor, pitched his run-off campaign to the theme that his black opponent, Tom Bradley, was in bond to a "minority bloc."

In 1962 Alabama, that sort of euphemism wasn't necessary. The rule of the game was that if a candidate carried the black precincts, he'd better win over fifty percent of the entire vote in the *first* primary and avoid a run-off. If he had to face a run-off, the fact that he was the choice of black voters would be used against him by his opponent—with a vengeance.

The term "Black Hand" came from the advertisement generally run by white supremacist candidates using the technique. It was an ad featuring a crude cartoon of a ballot box, with a black hand holding a ballot and poised over the drop-slit. In bold type beneath the cartoon, the legend read:

DON'T LET THE BLACK BLOC VOTE ELECT YOUR _____.

(Fill in the blank: "GOVERNOR" or "SENATOR" or "MAYOR" or "ATTORNEY GENERAL.")

At one time or another, the "Black Hand" had been used at every level of state and local government in the South by Seg candidates whose only chance for victory was to swing a large, frightened, white bloc majority to their side.

Within hours after vote results came in showing Flowers had carried the black boxes, his opposition went to the standard "Black Hand" attack. Racist handbills detailing returns from black precincts were circulated throughout Alabama by the hundreds of thousands. Newspaper advertisements were prepared carrying the same message. By word of mouth, Flowers was labeled the "niggers' candidate for Attorney General."

In 1962 Alabama, then in the process of electing George Wallace to his first term as governor on a "Segregation forever" platform, the theme had real possibilities. So they called me in from Washington, the prodigal son returned; not exactly in triumph, however. In fact, they stashed me like a hired gun in a motel on the outskirts of Montgomery, registered under an assumed name.

Odd, I thought, settling in with a pot of coffee and copies of the opposition's campaign material: in Alabama, I always seemed to be a broom-closet adviser.

Why? The old Jewish business again? Not exactly. You see, they explained, if word got out that a *Washington adviser* had been imported to work on the Flowers campaign, *I* could become the issue.

The PR counsel as the PR problem. I had half a notion

to settle for air fare back to Sodom-on-the-Potomac. But the challenge was too tempting. There I was, ensconced in the Cradle of the Confederacy with a gut full of corn bread and an idea on how Richmond Flowers could win a Southern election despite the handicap of black voter support in a first primary.

It could be done. But not, I knew from experience, by an appeal to voter reason. Or, God forbid, racial tolerance. No, what I had in mind was the obverse of Big Jim Folsom's Law of Pension Promises.

"The only way to beat a seventy-five-dollar a month pension promise," Big Jim once counseled his protegé, George Wallace, "is with an eighty-dollar a month pension promise."

The mirror image of this argument is that the best way to beat a hate is with a bigger hate.

The political PR man's job, you see, isn't always shaping public opinion. Sometimes it's shaping the client's image to what public opinion wants. Follow-the-followers.

This, then, is how a moderate candidate for public office responded to a racist attack in the Deep South, circa 1962. Under advice of his imported PR counsel.

Willard Livingston, Flowers' opponent, was the son of J. Edward Livingston, then Chief Justice of the Alabama Supreme Court. Until I arrived, Flowers' supporters had been trying to make the point, which I considered valid, that it would be improper for the chief law enforcement officer of the state (the Attorney General) to be the son of the chief judicial officer (the Chief Justice).

The argument, while it had logic and propriety on its side, was too amorphous to be a vote-grabber. Legal theorists found it impressive, but voters aren't always attracted by logic and propriety.

CASE STUDY: During the 1962 U.S. Senate race in

Massachusetts, Eddie McCormack built an entire campaign around the theme that Ted Kennedy's only qualification for office was being the brother of the President. Voters became convinced McCormack was right. They also figured that being the President's brother was a damned good qualification. Better, in fact, than being the nephew of the Speaker of the House, which was one of McCormack's chief qualifications. The same voter logic applied to Flowers' argument against a father-son team in the judicial law enforcement branch of Alabama state government, unless it was presented in a more jaundiced light.

One way to jaundice the light would have been to accuse the old Chief Justice of trying to practice nepotism. Nice dirty sound there: *nepotism.* Folk legend has it that George Smathers, JFK's best man at his wedding, used that line against Claude Pepper in 1950: ("He practices nepotism in Washington, and his sister is a thespian in New York!") But there were drawbacks to that line.

First, technically speaking, electing an official to an office who has a relative in another office isn't nepotism. More important, however, the nepotism line just wasn't strong enough to counter the Black Hand argument. Pound-for-pound in Alabama, 1962, a good nepotist would beat a good "nigger-lover" any day.

Beat a hate with a bigger hate, but handle with care. The trick isn't to be more racist than the opposition. Candidates under Black Hand attack who panicked and began shouting "Nigger!" to prove their Southern white heritage—in addition to whatever moral loss they sustained—drove their black supporters away from the polls.

Flowers didn't have any counterattack like that in mind. He was eyeing the governor's race four years in the future. Looking ahead, he correctly surmised that every

politician in Alabama would soon be wooing the then despised "Black bloc vote."

Rich was right—though he wouldn't be the man to
cash in on his early investment in moderation. By 1974,
even George Wallace was pumping black hands for votes.
But this was 1962, and "Segregation forever!" was still
the vogue. How could a moderate prosper in Seg-land?

The answer was in establishing guilt by free association. I worked on an advertisement that could exploit
some symbol of Southern regional frustration without
actually selling racial hostility. There was a thin line there.
But by the time I met with Flowers and his advisers a
few hours after arriving, I'd earned my fee. Provided, of
course, I could convince the client of that fact.

Presentation to the client is the most treacherous
part of the PR business. It's not enough to concoct
schemes and diversions to persuade the public. You have
to fight your way through your own ranks to get to the
public.

During my early PR days, I could hardly wait to
break a brainstorm over a client's head. Sometimes I'd
call one up at midnight and blurt, "Guess what I just
came up with . . ."

I soon learned, however, that some clients recoil
when the idea man they've hired comes on too strong,
too soon. The more daring and imaginative the idea, the
stronger the recoil. After scaring hell out of dozens of
clients with bold, daring proposals phoned in at midnight, I learned the trick of the Socratic sell. Questions-
and-answers, handwalking a client, step by step, through
my own thought process—until the idea became *his* idea.

I met Flowers and his campaign advisers in a downtown Montgomery hotel room, but before pulling the
draft advertisement from my coat pocket and laying it
open to general view, I played a quick game of Q-and-A.

"Let me ask you," I asked them. "If you had to draw up a list of the Five Most Despised National Figures in Alabama, who'd be on it?"

The two Kennedys, John and Bobby, were mentioned immediately (Teddy was then only a glint in Richard Daley's eye). Martin Luther King, Jr., came next. There followed a heated argument between two of Flowers' aides on whether Jacob Javits was more despised by Alabamians than Herbert Brownell, who still enjoyed a residual Hate Quotient from his days as Eisenhower's Attorney General.

Finally, there was Earl Warren, Chief Justice of the United States. About *him*, everybody agreed. Just as I'd figured. For this was the heart of IMPEACH EARL WARREN country. The man's name was anathema. I closed in for the sale.

"Suppose," I said, looking toward the candidate himself, who was laying back, detached from it all, as his advisers squabbled, "that Earl Warren, *Junior*—the Chief Justice's son, understand—became Attorney General of the United States?"

I waited a beat for the idea to register. Flowers, one of the quickest politicians I ever worked with, was the first man in the room to grab it. As it turned out, he wouldn't even have needed the Socratic sell.

"Father-and-son," he snapped. "Let's see it."

I handed him the layout. The rest gathered around his chair. Big bold print. A few well-chosen words. Right to the point.

Voters of Alabama

WOULD YOU WANT EARL WARREN, JUNIOR,
FOR U.S. ATTORNEY GENERAL?

Suppose Earl Warren's son became U.S. Attorney General? Far-fetched? Not at all. There are those in Alabama who want a FATHER-SON TEAM running the judicial and law enforcement branches of our state government. Block this plot to upset Alabama's traditional separation of powers. Go to the polls on June 5 and elect

RICHMOND FLOWERS/ATTORNEY GENERAL

It was one of the most demagogic political advertisements I ever created. But *enlightened* demagoguery, if I had to say so myself. Which I did, repeatedly, after the election results came in. Only I called it "demonstrative voter education."

Using Earl Warren's name in the ad was incidental, I later explained to my wife, Dale. She had a bad habit of pressing me about such matters. Why, we could have used the name of *any Chief Justice;* all I did was bring the voters a better understanding of the principle of separation of powers.

The irony of the ad made it sweeter to draft, of course. To identify an opponent running a racist campaign in Alabama in 1962 with, of all people, Earl Warren —that, along with the corn bread, was a hired gun's fringe benefit.

The Earl Warren, Jr., ad ran in major newspapers throughout Alabama during the last week of the campaign. I also scripted a special thirty-second radio spot with the same message. According to field reports, the Warren counterattack didn't actually swing votes away from Flowers' opponent. But it helped muck up the opposition's dichotomy of Black versus White.

Flowers was swept into office. The Black Hand was defeated—for the first time in Alabama political history. More irony: on the very same day, George Wallace, running his "stand-in-the-schoolhouse-door" campaign, won his first term as governor.

"Rich could be elected governor in four years," I

told one of his advisers as he drove me to the airport.

"Not a chance," he replied. "I hate to say it, but some of the same people who put him into office are gonna ruin him. I'm not talking about the Black Bloc vote, either. I mean—well, like the guy who put up the bread to bring you down here."

I never asked who that was. But I thought about it on the plane back to Sodom. And again, years later, when the man I helped elect chief law enforcement officer of Alabama was charged, tried, and convicted of official extortion. It was the kind of political problem no PR man, however expert, could remedy.

As I write these words, Spiro Agnew and John Mitchell look down benignly from a 1972 photo on my den wall. It shows them smiling from behind a mike-cluttered podium at something a short distance away and below their vantage point.

That something was me, on my haunches, barking at a covey of still photographers. I was telling them to clear the area in front of the podium so that the Vice President and Attorney General could proceed with their news conference. The site was the Old Indian Treaty Room of the Executive Office Building, next to the White House. The news conference concerned the formation of the Law Enforcement Assistance Administration, the Nixon White House election-year answer to the problem of crime in the streets.

The inscription on the photo is from Spiro Agnew. It reads: "Yes, Mr. Attorney General, that is the volatile, pugnacious Victor Gold—and I agree, he is a tough S.O.B."

I had met John Mitchell a few times before that day. But this was the first time he had ever met me. Let me explain . . .

The key to success in climbing the ladder of power

and prestige in Washington isn't really who-you-know, it's who-knows-you. I called it Selvage's Law (I have a law, rule, or corollary for everything, in case you hadn't figured it out by now). When Jim Selvage first considered leaving a comfortable job at the National Association of Manufacturers to form his own agency, he discussed the plan with an older friend.

"Where will you get your business?" the friend asked, as Selvage tells the story.

"Well, I've been with the NAM a long time now and know a lot of big men—chairmen of the board and company presidents," the younger Selvage replied. "I think I've got enough to go on."

"You know them, Jim," the elder counseled. "But the question is, do *they* know *you?* Get to that point, then open your PR office."

Mitchell and I had seen each other in social mob scenes on several occasions. He got word from time to time of my remarkable exploits antagonizing members of the national media on Spiro Agnew's behalf. I had, for example, gained particular note among high Administration officials when I told *Time* magazine that Maxine Cheshire, *The Washington Post* gossip columnist, had "the carapace of an armadillo."

Mitchell appreciated what I'd said, but very few others knew what the hell I was talking about, the penalty for polysyllabilizing in a monosyllabic Administration. (Look what they finally did to Agnew!) Bob Haldeman and Ron Ziegler didn't like it. But then, they never liked anything I did or said as Agnew's press secretary. Julie Nixon Eisenhower, however, approved of my assault on Maxine and even sought me out at one gathering to congratulate my "going after that . . ." Really, *dots.* The sentence just trailed off. Trust me. If Julie had called Maxine a _____, _____, or _____, I'd say so.

Anyway, Mitchell heard about me from Bryce Harlow, my old friend and political mentor who first recommended me to Agnew. But until that day in the Old Indian Treaty Room, the Attorney General had never witnessed my Press Secretary-as-Gauleiter act. That afternoon, I gave one of my finest performances and Mitchell was suitably awed. He hadn't heard of anything like it since Otto Dietrich was handling press for Hitler at the Reich-chancellery.

"YOU HAVE EXACTLY THREE MINUTES TO GET INTO FIXED POSITION WITH YOUR CAMERAS!" I shouted, about halfway up my usual decibel Richter scale of 10.

The Treaty Room was once used by Eisenhower for his Presidential news conferences, but it's too small for major press sessions by modern standards. When I arrived to handle press at the Agnew-Mitchell conference, the place looked like a media refugee camp, with three networks, two dozen still photographers, and thirty or forty print correspondents stumbling over their own equipment and notebooks.

The conference was scheduled for 2:00 P.M. But by 2:05 the still cameras were clicking away underneath the principals' armpits and television technicians were in a pushing and shoving and screeching contest for position in back of the room.

"THREE minutes!" I repeated.

"Whatsamatter, Vic, gettin' *soft?*" challenged Wally Mears, the AP man on the front row. "Five years ago you'da said *one* minute."

Young PR men should know that print men despise electronic men in the news media, and the sentiment is fervently reciprocated. The idea of a monolithic "media" is as out of date as that of a monolithic "Communist world."

On a superficial level, this print-electronic conflict can get an unknowing PR man in trouble simply for using the word "press" or "media" in the wrong company.

Gutenberg newspapermen claim the word "press" was good enough for the Founding Fathers (as in "freedom of the . . .") and they resent references to "the news media." On the other hand, television and radio correspondents dislike references to "members of the press."

Early in the Nixon years they succeeded in getting official terminology changed so that the President would have a "news secretary" and hold (or *not* hold, as it later developed) *"news conferences."*

Mears and other print reporters come to a news conference with their pencils poised and pads at the ready. That's all *they* need. Why, they figure, should a conference be delayed just to let their electronic competitors set up?

"TWO minutes!" I bellowed, turning at that point to see Mitchell in the act of calling Agnew to his side. The A-G nodded in my direction and said something to the Vice President, who smiled, nodded, and said something in return. Coincidentally, Karl Schumacher, an official White House photographer occasionally assigned to the Vice President, snapped a photo of the two men together at the podium.

"What was it you and Mitchell were talking about when you were looking over at me?" I asked Agnew.

"He asked me if that was Vic Gold, and when I said yes, he said, 'He sure is a tough sonofabitch.'"

And so I have that autographed photo on my den wall, showing two of America's most powerful leaders, at the zenith of their careers, gazing down bemusedly on what, for all the world knows, might have been the carapace of an armadillo.

Yet more came out of that first meeting with John Mitchell than a commendation for tough sonofabitchery. The incident stuck in his memory. When he took charge of the Committee to Re-elect the President, my name came up as just the man he wanted to head up the Nixon campaign's "attack group."

The "attack group" was set up as a political PR force composed of representatives from the White House and the Committee to Re-elect. Its purpose, as conceived, was to get the best political PR minds of the Nixon campaign together each day to formulate news media policy. It would decide what issues to stress in speeches and statements made by Nixon surrogates, as well as counter opposition attacks with a steady propaganda barrage. This would guarantee the Administration a dominant share of campaign news coverage, print and electronic alike.

An incumbent President enjoys an overwhelming edge in propaganda firepower during election year, even when he's seemingly holding himself "above" the political fray. Every time he announces a new program, or, as in 1972, a fresh peace initiative, a President both enhances his image and upstages the opposition's campaign. The "I'm too busy being President to run for the Presidency," or constitutional monarchial-style of campaigning, did not originate with Richard Nixon; he was emulating the style of Eisenhower in 1956 and Roosevelt in 1944. But Nixon had studied his predecessors' technique and in 1972, he applied it with a vengeance.

A citizen PR man's observation here: men in political life who wonder why the image of "politicians" is rated low by the public should consider the impact of campaigns by Presidents and other officeholders in which "politics" itself is depicted as being something to "rise above" if the "higher interest" is served.

Any time an incumbent—President, governor, or mayor—adopts a PR posture of being "above politics," it's a fundamental affront to the democratic process and he shouldn't be allowed to get away with it. The only known leaders in history "above politics" were kings, emperors, and dictators. If the Year of Watergate does nothing else, it will perhaps lay to rest that particular PR sham.

The 1972 "attack force" was part of the Nixon campaign's overall PR strategy. This plan consisted of keeping the President "above the battle," while using every available Administration propaganda resource to attack the opposition. Presidential surrogates, including the Vice President and Cabinet members, would carry the main weight of the attacks. The strategy was to keep the Democratic candidate debating lower-echelon spokesmen instead of his real opponent.

The strategy, as I say, did not originate with the Nixon campaign. It's an old gambit, designed to reduce the public image of the opposition as much as to enhance that of the incumbent.

In the 1972 Nixon campaign scheme, however, the underlying assumption was that some segments of the national news media would do everything possible to promote the Democratic candidate, whoever might be nominated—Muskie, McGovern, or, lurking in the back of everyone's mind during the early months of 1972, Ted Kennedy.

The "attack group" would also lead the Administration charge against hostile segments of the news media. Vice President Agnew would no longer be the White House pointman in that field. The 1972 script called for him to assume a new Mr. Nice Veep image, a low profile less likely to draw fire from either the opposition or news media.

Mitchell wanted me to be chief coordinator between the official White House propaganda team and the Committee to Re-elect's PR staff. "Coordinator" is a bureaucratic euphemism meaning that a particular job can be whatever its holder wants it to be and/or is able to make of it.

Mitchell was looking for a take-charge type. What he probably had in mind—I say this, reflecting on what the Watergate exposés revealed about conflicts within the President's own circle—was to put his own man into a key position on the "attack force." Maybe to keep an eye on his rival, Charles Colson.

Colson was a Massachusetts lawyer who, though lacking any professional experience or aptitude for the assignment, emerged as Nixon's No. 1 PR adviser from 1970 to 1972. The Bostonian's chief virtue as a Presidential PR consultant was that he reinforced Nixon's own idea that he didn't need a PR consultant, being more expert in the field than the experts around him.

Colson's ascendancy as Nixon's PR alter-ego led to some sticky moments in the Vice President's press office, as when the President's representative would call to "suggest" an idea that Agnew might use in a speech. Such last-minute Presidential brainstorms were expected to be thrown into Agnew speeches as "inserts," regardless of whether they had anything to do with the main subject matter of the address.

On one occasion when he was infuriated at AFL-CIO President George Meany's Democratic partisanship, Nixon decided to dramatize a link between Meany and Ed Muskie, then front-runner for the Democratic Party's Presidential nomination. Colson came to Agnew's office to suggest that the Vice President, in a speech to be delivered the following day at Miami Beach, label Muskie and

Meany "the M & M Twins." He thought the idea was so good that he'd even done us the favor of preparing a draft "insert" of the line.

In his time, Agnew bought a good many White House-prepared alliterations. But this one melted in his hand, not in his mouth. He told Colson he'd have to think it over. Then, after the President's aide left the office, I was instructed to "fluff that one"— Agnew's way of ordering me to derail an idea without appearing to turn down a direct Presidential request.

I called Colson and told him that having looked the speech over from a dozen different angles, it was hard to see how the "M & M Twins" line, magnificent as it was, could be squeezed in.

"Too bad," he muttered. "It would make the Old Man happy."

(The Old Man, in the argot of Colson's pecking order, was the President. Among Vice Presidential staff members, inner-office code labeled Nixon as "Hertz," our own leader as "Avis.")

I apologized, but eagerly suggested an alternative. Secretary of the Treasury Connally was going on the *Today* show the following morning. If he were to use the line at that time it would get immediate national coverage, far greater than as an insert in an Agnew speech. Fluff mission completed. Colson turned his (or was it Hertz's?) idea over to Connally, who unleashed it next morning. The Old Man, presumably, was happy. For that news cycle, at least.

As the '72 campaign progressed, Colson proliferated such ideas with manic zest. The most manic was for Agnew to charge that McGovern's statements about Viet Nam peace efforts "bordered on treason." Since that proposal was made to Agnew when the public opinion polls showed Nixon with a 30 percent lead over his opponent, it seemed a little excessive. I told Avis that if he issued the statement after all the media talk about "the new Agnew," it would undo three months of his own careful image-repairing.

The Vice President agreed. Nevertheless, he said, there was no choice: "The President wants this."

"I can't believe that," I said. "I can't believe the President himself could think something like this would do any good.'" (Actually, I *could* believe it. But I also thought that if the idea were kicked back to the White House, whatever wild hair was growing when the statement was prepared might have been removed by that time.)

Agnew took the statement up with Haldeman, who called back to say on reconsideration, Agnew was right. The statement was really meant for Someone Else. Whoever Someone Else turned out to be escapes my memory. But it must have been some surrogate so far down the line that he couldn't make the newswires. In any case, I never heard mention of McGovern's "treason" again.

Regardless of his brash ineptitude as a political PR specialist, Colson had the President's ear. Or rather, the President had his. This meant that Colson would be the dominant voice at "attack force" meetings. Mitchell, who had come to resent Colson's sudden rise as a Presidential political adviser, might have had other ideas.

The first hint I got of being considered to "coordinate" the "attack group" came in an odd way. It was at a political fund-raiser where Agnew was the featured speaker. The Vice President had just begun his talk to Republican fatcat contributors, who had paid $500 to $1000 to eat cold roast beef and drink hot gin and tonics on an old Maryland plantation.

The press had not been invited. Fatcats generally don't care for publicity regarding their political largesse. So I was fairly relaxed, leaning up against a magnolia tree, sipping straight gin and enjoying the Maryland countryside. I flashed Red Alert only after realizing that the heavy, bejowled presence who had come up alongside was His Eminence, Martha's husband. She wasn't on the premises, however. He also appeared fairly relaxed.

"We're going to put you to work in the President's campaign," John Mitchell said, low-pitched, out of the side of his mouth.

My initial reaction was that he was rebuking me for lolling on the job. "Really?" I answered. I pointed toward Agnew: "I'm already working. For that fella up there. The one speaking."

It wasn't a flip answer. Mitchell was a formidable authority figure. Not frightening, just awesome. You talk and listen to such people the way Dorothy did to the Wizard—until someone pulls aside the curtain. Which, as of early 1972, hadn't happened in John Mitchell's case.

"We'll take care of that," Mitchell said. "We need you for a tough job. I hear you're the toughest sonofabitch in town."

I thanked him for the compliment, but said that there were others much tougher. Naming, for openers, my friend, Lyn Nofziger, who had been Ronald Reagan's communications director and later worked for the Nixon White House.

"Nofziger?" Mitchell asked, drawing on his pipe. "Well yeah, he's tough, but tough and fat. You're tough and *lean*." He rapped my rib cage. "We'll be in touch."

I reported the conversation to Agnew, who looked perplexed. He was sweating out the Vice Presidential renomination question. Hertz seemed to enjoy the game of

Let-Him-Sweat. It seemed peculiar, if not significant, that the President's political manager would make an offer of future employment to the Vice President's press secretary.

I told Agnew that I intended to turn down Mitchell's offer.

"You understand, I don't have the slightest idea whether I'll be back on the ticket," he said.

"Well, if you're not, it won't make any difference anyway," I replied. "I won't work for Nixon-Connally."

Agnew shrugged.

"We'll go up or down together," I said.

The good, loyal PR man. I meant it. It didn't make any sense to me that Nixon would dump Agnew for John Connally, although I once heard Agnew himself say that this was what the man in the Oval Office would have liked to do. Still, if that were to happen, I wouldn't want to stick around. I had never been much of a Nixon man. Nixon and Connally on the same ticket would have put me on Maalox for the duration.

So I turned down the Mitchell offer and waited for word on whether the ticket was again going to be Nixon-Agnew. It finally came. The man who brought the message to the Vice President was John Mitchell. Pete Malatesta made a note of the date: June 16, 1972.

Memorable date: the last day of pre-Watergate American history. On the following night, June 17, eight men were arrested for breaking-and-entering Democratic National Committee headquarters. All hired, one way or another, through John Mitchell's office. Some fat, some lean, but taken together eight of the toughest sons of bitches any Presidential campaign manager could ask for.

173

10. Jerry Ford, Where Am I Now That You Need Me?

We'll have a speech straight: come give us a taste of your quality; come, a passionate speech.

Hamlet's PR advice to the Players (II. ii.)

———◆———

There are two genres of PR men: lapel-strokers and writing hacks.

Strokers are social types who "get along well with people" while working the corridors of power—corporate board rooms, Capitol Hill lobbies, editorial offices. They "engineer consent" (Bernay's phrase) by word of mouth. Many, if not a majority, of these strokers are functional illiterates, their highest literary form being the cliché-larded memorandum talked into a dictograph.

Strokers account for most of the general public misconception about working public relations. Every young Willie Loman with a smile-and-a-shoeshine believes he's qualified to be a PR man because he can "get along." Yet the truth of the matter is that the best PR men I ever knew—me, for one, and my first employer, Sam Bledsoe—hardly got along with anyone we worked with, either client or office associates.

174

But then, we weren't lapel strokers. Selvage & Lee would not even trust Sam alone in a board room with a client. The New York office was afraid of what the head of their Washington office might say that could unhinge an account. Too candid, you see. Like the time, back in the 1930s when Henry Wallace dispatched Sam to represent him at a White House Cabinet meeting.

Wallace was then Franklin Roosevelt's Secretary of Agriculture. Bledsoe served as his top PR adviser. One morning the Secretary couldn't make a Cabinet meeting, so Sam filled in. For the first and the last time.

Roosevelt had a bright idea on how to solve some economic problem. A Presidential brainstorm had come to him in the middle of the night. He spelled it out, then went around the table soliciting Cabinet comments. FDR began with his Secretary of Treasury, Henry Morgenthau, whom he referred to as "Rabbi."

Morgenthau thought the President's idea was just dandy, an opinion shared by most of the other Cabinet members. A few withheld judgment, saying they would have to check certain aspects of the problem before making up their minds. Then came the Department of Agriculture's turn.

Bledsoe is a fast-talking west Tennessean, which sometimes makes his conversation difficult to follow. It's like listening to a 33⅓ rpm Ozark hill accent running at 78 rpm. That morning he rattled off half a dozen specific objections to the Roosevelt plan before the secretary of the Cabinet broke in to remind a frowning President that since His Excellency had an 11:00 A.M. appointment the Cabinet meeting would have to move along.

Next day, Henry Wallace called in his PR chief to ask what he had done to trigger a late-night phone call from a White House staff assistant telling him never to send that "crazy sonofabitch" Bledsoe to a Cabinet meeting again. The rule, about which Wallace had neglected to advise Bledsoe, was that when attending Roosevelt Cabinet meetings you either went along with the President or kept your mouth shut. Which leads us to Berle's Criterion: Adolph, not Milton.

Adolph Berle, one of the bright young men of the Roosevelt Administration, made a virtue of this kind of sycophancy. The primary requisite for a good White House staff man, said Berle, was "a passion for anonymity."

Uneuphemized: don't make waves. Blend into the woodwork. If there's credit to be passed out for a White House policy, the President gets it. If there's blame, it's never the President's fault. "They" did it.

Who are "they"? "They" are the self-effacing sycophants around Presidents who, whenever He makes a bad decision, get the blame. The word goes out that They "misled Him" or "let Him down."

It's all part of the President-Can-Do-No-Wrong syndrome. To criticize a Presidential policy while you're on the White House payroll is considered at best, prima donnaism, at worst, treachery. This was true during the Nixon-Agnew years. It's likely to remain true, no matter who moves into the White House, so long as little men working around Big Men enjoy the perquisites that go with their jobs.

Still, while Berle's Criterion hasn't changed in forty years, the principle of anonymity has suffered some erosion in the area of speechwriting. Ghosts have gone public, possessed by a demonic passion for notoriety. Since the Eisenhower years, Presidential speeches have lacked only a printed byline to establish their true authorship.

The list of Presidential speechwriters imbued with

this passion includes Emmett John Hughes and Malcolm Moos under Eisenhower; Ted Sorensen and Dick Goodwin under Kennedy; Bill Moyers under Johnson; and Bill Safire, Ray Price, Jim Keogh and Pat Buchanan under Nixon; Bob Hartmann under Ford.

In my early days as Spiro Agnew's press secretary, I was a devout believer in Berle's passion for anonymity, particularly as it applied to writing speeches for public figures. This reflected my PR training, it being a truism of the trade that people prefer political leaders who utter their own words when speaking.

Ask any American for an off-the-cuff impression of how a President ought to go about preparing a public address and what you'll get is the Lincoln story: the lonely figure in a stovepipe hat and shawl scribbling out his classic address en route to the speech site.

It makes a good tale, but from my own experience with Republican politicians, I doubt its authenticity. The Gettysburg Address had to go through at least five drafts —with three inserts put in at the suggestion of Cabinet members, friendly Congressmen, and the chairman of the Pennsylvania State Republican Committee—before Lincoln even got out of the Washington train station.

The only political client I ever knew who actually scribbled a speech out on the back of an envelope was Spiro Agnew. The occasion was the Midwinter Republican Governors Conference, February, 1971. The results were disastrous.

Theoretically, Agnew's mission at the conference was to salve the wounds of Republican governors who were unseated in November, 1970. But because he had been chairman of the Governors Conference during his tenure as governor of Maryland, Agnew thought he knew his audience well enough to speak without a prepared text.

On the trip from Washington to the speech site, however, something happened which, as Agnew's PR man, I should have been able to anticipate: my client read that morning's edition of *The New York Times*. Now, letting a copy of *The New York Times* fall into Spiro Agnew's hands en route to a speech was gross professional negligence. It invariably produced great fires in the client's belly, conflagrations that could only be extinguished by a torrent of words.

On this occasion there was a *Times* dispatch on the Governors Conference written by R. W. (Johnny) Appel. Appel reported the reaction of certain Republican governors to Agnew's role in the 1970 election. Within minutes, Agnew's viscus was flaring. He slipped out an envelope and began scribbling furiously. Twenty minutes later he handed his neo-Gettysburg masterpiece across the plane aisle.

Have you ever tried to read a masterpiece in scrawl at 35,000 feet above sea level? My own visceral reaction was that Agnew's speech was indecipherable. But playing a PR hunch that any address written on the back of an envelope by an American politician couldn't be all bad, I nodded my approval.

"Looks great to me," I said. Actually, as I later learned when Agnew delivered it, the speech wasn't bad. Delivered at another time and place, it might even have been given high grades in forensic excellence. But as a *political* speech at that time and place, it was terrible. Agnew was about to make the mistake of trying to lecture his audience. To tell the governors what they didn't want to hear.

This was exactly what wasn't called for at the Republican Governors Conference of February, 1971. The 1970 elections, held only two months before, had decimated the lot. Lame ducks limped web-footed from meeting to meeting, stopping in corridors to complain to any nearby member of the press corps or hotel cleaning force that they had been royally screwed by the Nixon White House and their national party. It was a grim political land-scape, a dramatic contrast to the stunning natural scenery all around.

Governors, Republicans and Democrats alike, always schedule their national and regional conferences at sites where they can put their collective fingers on the pulse of the country's most urgent problems. They go to the hotbeds of American urban-industrial trouble—places like San Juan, Lake Tahoe, and Colonial Williamsburg.

Sun Valley, Idaho, was the site of the 1971 Midwinter Republican Governors Conference. Only coincidentally, of course, the conference happened to fall at the height of the ski season. And by some stroke of luck, many of the governors in attendance and their wives had thought to pack their skis in with their skivvies.

Still, three days on the slopes weren't enough to im-prove the dispositions of the numerous outgoing governors who were present. They seethed beneath their parkas and waited to pounce on a contingent of party speakers flying in from Washington.

First came Congressman Rogers Morton, then Re-publican National Chairman. Morton, a hulking man, looks like a sympathetic St. Bernard in search of a lost brandy flask. Even if he hadn't uttered a word, the party chairman's normally doleful expression was exactly what the occasion demanded. And by the time he'd finished, his lame-duck listeners were properly reassured that (just as they suspected all along) their being separated from the public payroll was the worst catastrophe to befall any Western country since Dunkirk.

179

Morton's mea culpa was a tough act to follow. But then, in breezed Spiro Agnew, with that speech scrawled on the back of an envelope. No mea culprit, he. If you've lost your governorship, Agnew said in effect, stop whining. Don't expect any sympathy from me. Get off your asses and shape up for the next election. Any questions?

"Has he lost his *mind?*" John Lindsay (the *Newsweek* correspondent, not the New York politician) asked me after the speech was finished and the audience had stumbled out of the hall into the midnight snow, shaking their fists toward the cold black Idaho sky.

"No, just spoken it," I said.

"Well," said Lindsay, an astute Irish observer of political affairs, "next time tell him not to present the bill for the funeral while the wake's still going on."

Agnew's shot-from-the-hip Envelope Address at the 1971 Midwinter Republican Governors Conference had its irony, because few politicians ordinarily spent as much time and effort preparing and stylizing their speeches.

Most politicians these days are indifferent to the discipline of good speechmaking, in fact. They pick up good honoraria for addressing convention and club audiences around the country, but hardly bother to look at their texts before dashing off to National Airport to catch a plane to the speaking site.

The speeches are usually given a once-over while the speaker sips a bourbon or Scotch in flight. But there are instances in which the material isn't inspected even up to the moment the speaker is introduced and spreads his text across the lectern.

This practice can lead to some bad speeches for good honoraria. It can even lead to non-speeches. Which is what happened when Senator Joseph Montoya, the Senate Watergate committee's most forgettable inquisitor, rushed to the platform of the National Legislative Conference in Albuquerque, mid-August, 1974.

Following the general PR practice, Montoya's staff had prepared both a speech and a newspaper-style release summarizing the speech's highlights. Now came a demonstration of how the PR tail can wag the dog. At the lectern, the speaker pulled out his material and began reading *not* his prepared remarks, but the advance news summary!

"For Immediate Release!" Montoya barked, snapping a half-stunned, half-stoned audience to attention. "Senator Joseph Montoya, Democrat of New Mexico, last night told the National Legislative Conference meeting at Albuquerque that . . ."

Speakers who don't read their texts in advance are bad enough, but a speaker who doesn't listen to himself reading it? I felt for the Senator's PR man. Unbelievably, Montoya continued right through to the end of his six-page release, stumbling only in befuddled reaction to catcalls from his listeners. Audience protests were especially loud when the speaker, reading from his advance release, declared that "Montoya was repeatedly interrupted by applause during the course of his remarks."

While the Montoya episode isn't typical of anything but Joseph Montoya, it does reflect an extreme form of the malaise that afflicts modern American oratory. Read through a copy of the Congressional Record, if you can stand it. What you'll find are the words of men seeking political safety in oratorical homogeneity.

Gerald Ford is the foremost representative of this modern Nasal Banal School of Political Oratory.

I ghosted several speeches for Ford in 1967, when he was House Republican leader with an eye out for bigger and better things. That's right: regardless of what you might have heard about Jerry the Reluctant President, the truth is that he was thinking of Jerry and Betty at 1600 Pennsylvania Avenue even then.

Goldwater's 1964 debacle had left the Republican party in disarray. The 1968 Presidential nomination seemed up for grabs. Richard Nixon, still a private citizen practicing law in New York, was looked on by many Republicans as a political has-been.

Shortly after Ford unseated old Joe Martin as House Republican leader, he was encouraged by friends to look for professional talent that could help him build a national image. I was touted as a PR man who might help him in the speechwriting area. Another young Republican speechwriter recommended at the same time was Steve Hess, who later went to work at the White House during the first Nixon administration.

"What can you tell me about Steve Hess?" Ford asked one afternoon. "Dick Nixon's recommended him to me as a speechwriter. Didn't he have something to do with Goldwater's campaign speeches?"

Ford was confusing Steve Hess with Karl Hess, a common mistake around Washington in those days. Karl Hess had served as the chief Goldwater wordsmith during the '64 campaign. He won distinction by claiming authorship of the self-destruct line in Goldwater's acceptance speech at the convention: "Extremism in the defense of liberty is no vice, moderation in the pursuit of justice is no virtue."

The line was winning ideology but losing politics. It has generally been credited with blowing the Goldwater campaign before the candidate left the convention hall.

Considering that, Karl Hess' admission that he fathered such a line might be viewed as an act of unparalled candor for a political ghost-writer. Yet, what's really odd about Hess' claim is that he didn't originate the "extremism" line. It was plugged into Goldwater's acceptance speech by one Harry Jaffa, a sometime *National Review* contributor and conservative ideologue who teaches out West.

So why would Hess, or anybody, want to take dubious credit for one of the biggest speechwriting gaffes in Presidential history? One answer is that the passion for notoriety runs especially strong in some ghost egos.

In any case, I assured Congressman Ford that Steve Hess and Karl Hess weren't related by either blood or ideology. Steve Hess was a liberal Republican. Karl, a libertarian conservative during his Goldwater years, later flipped into the ranks of the New Left. He was last seen sculpting a bust of Frantz Fanon and eating sunflower seeds aboard a houseboat floating down the Severn River.

Steve Hess and I, Republican Left and Right working in tandem, each made a pass at writing speeches for our new House Minority Leader. Whatever our differences in political philosophy, we were both experienced on the national scene. We hoped to contribute to the molding of a new Ford image.

Could this be the Making of the President, 1968? In assessing Gerald Ford's potential as a Presidential candidate, the most impressive point in his favor back then was the fact that he'd risen to leadership among his House colleagues. But viewed through a PR prism, the man had obvious drawbacks. I was depressed by his lack of charisma. I recalled, however, that when John Kennedy first announced his candidacy for President, I hadn't been overly impressed with his magnetism, either.

For his part, Ford, while outgoing on most subjects, was coy whenever anyone mentioned the 1968 nomination. All he cared about, said the House Minority Leader, was electing a Republican Congress. That would have made him Speaker of the House.

One morning, however, Ford's protective veil parted slightly. He summoned me to Capitol Hill. When I arrived at his office he was looking over a copy of that morning's *Washington Post*. What had drawn his interest was a public opinion survey showing Chuck Percy with a 2 percent rating on a Presidential preference chart.

"How could Chuck Percy register *any* percent in a Presidential poll?" Ford asked. "Outside of Illinois, who's even heard of him?"

"Are you asking how an unknown quantity gets himself listed as a Presidential possibility?" I asked. "Or are you asking me how *you* can get listed?"

It was a leading question. Ford waved it aside.

"Just tell me how Chuck Percy rates a two percent," he replied.

"It's like this," I explained. "You put up a few thousand bucks for a national sampling of what people think of Chuck Percy—or Jerry Ford—as a Presidential possibility. The survey organization puts your name on a list. They show the list to fifteen hundred people. If thirty check your name, you've got two percent. Chuck Percy, Jerry Ford—anybody."

"And they put *that* in the papers?" Ford asked.

"Well, understand, it's a *private* survey," I said. "In addition to their newspaper columns the big public-opinion outfits all operate independent public-opinion services. They'll take a private survey for anything legitimate. If I gave them ten thousand bucks they'd take a Presidential preference survey for Vic Gold."

"I don't think you'd get two percent," Ford said.

"No, but I'd probably be listed among 'Others'," I replied. "Suppose, though, *you* had a private survey taken.

You'd show up with two to five percent. It would be a private poll. But I wouldn't be a bit surprised if it were published in one of your private pollster's newspaper columns."

Ford never worked up funds for a private survey of the kind I suggested. But that discourse on Chuck Percy's 2 percent Presidential rating was my major contribution to his understanding of politics beyond Grand Rapids and the House floor.

I certainly didn't upgrade the quality of his speeches, but neither did Steve Hess. We both learned that Gerald Ford didn't really want his oratory upgraded. At the moment of truth, when the final speech draft hit his desk, he invariably fled from any suggestion of high or stylish rhetoric.

In this respect, Ford is typical of the politicians of his age. At least, the white politicians, no invidious racial comparisons intended. In the opinion of this ghost-writer, most of America's great political orators over the past quarter-century have been black.

The greatest of all—black, white, or red—was Martin Luther King, Jr. Not in terms of what he said, understand. Rather, the way he said it. King's "I Have a Dream" speech was in the finest tradition of the great orators. It didn't *inform* people. It *moved* them.

Because of their oratorical training ground—churches with audiences that expect to be moved—black orators like King aren't afraid to reach for the emotional word, phrase, or cadence.

Chamber of Commerce-oriented white politicians, on the other hand, are generally suspicious of words that reflect drama or emotion in public places. Most modern American politicians reflexively blue-pencil such words and phrases when they turn up in speech drafts. This instinct, in my experience, is especially strong among conservative Republicans who have been trained since infancy to believe that a raised voice or waved arm is a sign of poor breeding. The middle-class PR rulebook emphasizes "dignity." This precludes any intonation of word or gesture that might suggest rabble-rousing.

I think that Barry Goldwater, a man of deep political commitment and passion, was cursed with this hang-up by his Anglican forebears. No matter how hot the words on a page, Goldwater always stayed cool. At times in 1964, watching the candidate word-walk a speech in front of an audience that ached to raise hell, I would hope that Goldwater, just once, would whip off his coat, roll up his sleeves, and let fly.

My parting of the ways as a ghost-writer for Gerald Ford was amicable. I just stopped pursuing speech assignments in his office and his office stopped pursuing me. But not before I'd written a stem-winder, complete with a dozen super-patriotic quotations straight out of J. Donald Adams' *Great Quotations* (a pocketbook, much better than *Bartlett's*, though not as good as the *Viking Book of Aphorisms*—but more about that later.)

The stem-winder was scheduled for delivery to an Eastern Europe anti-Communist Captive Nations group. Looking for the widest possible news coverage, I talked to Ford about departing from the standard hack text denouncing Communism-behind-the-Iron-Curtain. (Flack's note: the semantics used here are those of a pre-Kissinger Cold War era.)

My recommendation was that Ford take-a-ride on a more topical, newsworthy anti-Communist theme: attack Fidel Castro, who was still hot copy at the time. We could, of course, mesh in appropriate references to East European Communist regimes. But by concentrating on a Communist hate symbol closer to home, we would have a better crack at good coverage.

Ford bought the idea so I got down to work. The finished speech was vintage Gold Hackery. It was spiced with thundering invective, rolling cadences, and a dollop of inspirational quotes. The transitions were carefully worked out, cliché to cliché, with periodic escalations of word and phrase designed to excite, then bring the audience to a roaring climax.

By climax, let me say, I mean just that. The relationship between a good speaker and his audience, in my view, is one of seducer and seducee. A speech, after all, is a symbolic political sex act, you see. You don't? Well, let me explain . . .

First, there's the foreplay: a preliminary warm-up in which the speaker softens his audience with ingratiating remarks or light humor.

Then comes first contact with the subject matter: move slowly at this point to bring the audience to the sofa without jolting its sensibilities.

Then comes the body of the speech itself, with the speaker building audience response to a peak until, finally —what else?

Orgasm, if the speech is good and the speaker does his job. Meaning, an audience left standing and cheering, fulfilled in every expectation. And the speaker left limp and ready for a nightcap.

This technique varies, of course, depending on the size and intimacy of an audience. Including the most intimate audience of all, the television viewer.

There is no known case of orgasm having been achieved by a speaker to a TV audience (although Agnew came close in his Des Moines speech attacking the media in November, 1969). People seated in their living rooms have been known, however, to be stirred to a limited degree of vocal assent ("Yeah, you tell 'em!"), or even to be seduced to the point of sending in campaign contributions. But experience has shown that television as a communications aphrodisiac leaves something to be desired.

In candor, my Captive Nations speech for Jerry Ford wasn't a star-flashing exercise in oratorical copulation. But it was good enough to leave the audience aroused and somewhat spent, if properly delivered. I counted ten cheer lines and one, maybe two, standing ovations (apart from the opening and closing).

The operative phrase here is "if properly delivered." A dedicated speechwriter—even a hack—deserves a client who's willing to read over the material, rehearse it, and consider nuances like phrasing and voice inflection. In short, meet the text halfway.

This wasn't Ford's dish, however. At least, not in those years. He called me into his office to say that the content of the speech was fine, but the sentences were *too long!* I never argued with a speaker about style, since he was the man in the bullshit ring. But I was puzzled by Ford's request for "shorter" sentences.

"You mean they're unreadable?" I asked. "Some problem in breath control?"

"No," he replied, "I'm just used to shorter sentences in my speeches, that's all."

"But this is a foreign policy speech," I objected, "and a foreign policy speech needs a certain *tone,* you know? Tone doesn't come in salami slices."

"I didn't say anything about salami," Ford replied. "All I want is shorter sentences. *Understand?*"

A certain peevish note had come into his voice, unusual for Jerry Ford. But as I picked up those blood-stirring pages and headed out the door for the nearest salami-slicing machine, one last shot seemed in order.

"You know, Jerry," I said, "if you want to project a national image, sooner or later you're going to have to handle longer sentences."

"Maybe so," he smiled. "But for now, make 'em shorter."

So I went to the outer office, seated myself behind a typewriter, and sliced my fine cadences, rhythms, and quotations into neat wedges of verbal salami. Ford delivered the speech with sufficient verve to get half a dozen interruptions and a nice round of applause at the end. But no orgasm, of course.

That was ten years ago. A lot has happened to Jerry Ford since. For one thing, he's moved right along in Public Speaking 101. Not only does he deliver speeches composed of sentences in the fifteen- to twenty-word range. He's also worked on *tone* by acquiring the knack of Quotesmanship. Not just Straight Quotesmanship, either. *Learned* Quotesmanship.

Straight Quotesmanship is a standard speechwriter device to fill time and space in a dull text. A Straight Quote thrown into a speech isn't necessarily aimed at enhancing the client's image. Sometimes it simply reinforces a point or gets a speaker off the stage on what sounds like an upbeat, inspirational note.

Such as: ending speeches by quoting Thomas Jefferson, Franklin Roosevelt, John F. Kennedy (but *not* Lyndon B. Johnson) for a Democratic client addressing a Democratic audience. Or quoting Abraham Lincoln, Teddy Roosevelt, Dwight Eisenhower (but *not* Warren G. Harding) for a Republican client addressing a Republican audience.

For mixed bag audiences, any of the Founding Fathers—Washington, Madison, Monroe, Franklin (George Mason in the South)—are safe Straight Quotes. Alexis de Tocqueville is also very big on the circuit (but make sure your client has the name phonetically spelled in his speech text).

For speakers who don't mind moving out of the area of political Straight Quotesmanship, there are always Rudyard Kipling and Ralph Waldo Emerson (but be wary of Thoreau). Or popular sports figures, such as "Bear" Bryant, the late Vince Lombardi, and, for a laugh, Casey Stengel. Among black athletes, "Satchel" Paige is safe, Muhammad Ali is out when speaking before white audiences (though, when addressing a black audience, the reverse may be true).

For a Straight Quote to be politically failsafe before all audiences, the person being quoted ought to have been dead for at least a half-century. Lincoln, for example, is now quotable in the Deep South. Richard Nixon claimed that Woodrow Wilson was one of his favorite Presidents. Yet, only twenty years ago, Wilson's name wouldn't have been touched by a Republican politician with a ten-foot public opinion poll.

The carriage trade PR skill, however, lies in the ability to lace speeches with Learned Quotes. These are the image-enhancing literary and historical references designed to project the speaker as a man of heavy intellectual substance.

Learned Quotesmanship was one of Adlai Stevenson's two great contributions to modern American political discourse. The second was humor. Before Stevenson came onto the national scene in 1952, PR men advised politicians to shun public displays of intellectuality or wit.

Stevenson (our best *white* political orator of the past

Jerry Ford, Where Am I Now That You Need Me?

half-century) was criticized for alienating voters by "talking over people's heads" and "cracking wise" in public.

But although Stevenson was twice smashed at the polls by one of the great non-stylists of American political oratory, the Illinois governor revolutionized the business of ghost speechwriting in this country. He was the pioneer who risked the worst—quoting Disraeli, Andrew Oliver, Bernard Shaw, and *The London Times* during a single noontime speech in Los Angeles!

Imitators of varying ability followed—from the Kennedys to, of all people, Jerry Ford.

The Kennedys were the first to mass-produce Learned Quotes out of Bartlett's, Adams' *Great Quotations, The Viking Book of Aphorisms,* and selections from *The World's Great Thinkers.*

Between 1956 and 1969, John Kennedy succeeded in altering his image from that of a playboy Senator to that of an intellectual heavyweight by larding speeches with as many as fifteen esoteric quotations in one twenty-minute clip.

Bobby Kennedy, who once had the image of a ruthless political operator, underwent his oratorical imagectomy at the skilled hands of a covey of egghead speechwriters, headed by his Senate aide, Adam Walinsky. By 1968, Bobby was quoting Camus and Aeschylus in speeches before college audiences.

In fact, Kennedy's frequent use of a quotation from the Greek playwright led Senator Eugene McCarthy (a genuine intellectual who didn't need a quotation book for his literary references) to charge Bobby with "Aeschylating" the 1968 campaign for the Democratic Presidential nomination. It was a line worthy of Stevenson. That is, it went right over the collective heads of McCarthy's audiences.

191

Stevenson took a risk flaunting intellectuality and wit in public speeches. But the Kennedys proved that Learned Quotesmanship was a successful PR tool. By the early 1970s, the most staid old-school politicians were playing Learned Quotesmanship.

Even Short-Sentence Jerry. After Nixon appointed him Vice President, Ford's first concession to his new national political status came when he stuck a toe in the Pierian spring, by quoting the fourteenth-century Arab historian-philosopher Ibn Khaldun to a convention of the Manufacturing Chemists Association.

Ibn Khaldun? Not ibn Bobby Kennedy would have risked that one. At least, not in the middle of the Arab oil boycott.

Learned Quotesmanship, clearly, is a fine word-tailor's art. It has to be suited to a speaker's style. You can't stick a Savile Row suit on a Robert Hall body.

But there are other forms of Quotesmanship, wholesale erudition to fit any customer. Total Quotesmanship, for example, as practiced in Senate filibusters.

In late summer, 1965, I was hired by a major industrial association to grind out filibuster speech copy for Everett Dirksen, the soporific Senate Republican leader. Dirksen was leading an "extended debate," i.e., euphemism for filibuster, against an AFL-CIO sponsored amendment to eliminate Section 14-b—the so-called "Right to work" amendment—from the Taft-Hartley law.

Since the purpose of a Senator filibuster is to kill time, the speechwriter does himself a favor simply by lifting material wholesale. Dirksen had a unique speaking style (given to such flourishes as calling a "birthday" a "natal anniversary"). But it wasn't called for in this case. All that's needed for filibuster speeches is Basic Drone.

So we had fun. As long as our material was "germane" to the debate, anything went. And it did, from my office to Dirksen's, in truckload quotes—Burke, Locke, Rousseau, and, of course, Jefferson, Madison, Monroe, Lincoln, Gompers, Georges Sorel . . . *Georges Sorel?* Check that; definitely not Georges Sorel or Frantz Fanon, either. But every kitchen sink and its kid brother were thrown into Ev Dirksen's "germane" remarks, *in toto*. All given due credit, of course. ("As the esteemed Justice Cardozo once wrote in an opinion rendered . . .")

I ground out 450 pages in three days! *Three days!* Or rather, Lisa Brown, my secretary, ground it out, since the most creative part of producing filibuster copy lies in the typing thereof.

The filibuster was successful, but neither Mrs. Brown nor I ever got so much as a thank you note from Ev Dirksen. No hard feelings, though. After all, he didn't even know I'd written his material. It was, you see, an assignment in which I was a Ghost-with-Cover.

Ghosting-with-Cover is writing speeches under conditions in which the speechmaker himself doesn't know whose copy he's reading. My client, the industrial association, was funneling copy to filibustering Senators whose own staffs were too limited to grind out all the material needed to keep the talkathon going. Dirksen's staff didn't care who was turning it out, just so the copy didn't quote Georges Sorel or Frantz Fanon.

Obviously, Ghosting-with-Cover tends to produce more oratorical dross than substance. But even dross-production can pose challenges for a speechwriter.

During the 1960 Presidential campaign, for example, I ghosted statements for both John Kennedy and Richard Nixon on the same issue. Both candidates, campaigning in

West Virginia coal mine country, came out in favor of a national fuels policy, a proposal then being pushed by the coal industry.

Naturally, the statements had to say the same thing. Our client wasn't paying us to open a national debate on the issue. But, obviously, it had to be said in different ways.

I didn't try to emulate the respective styles of Kennedy and Nixon; the material, after all, was whistle-stop stuff. Two minutes of insert aimed at local coal-mining audiences, telling them what they wanted to hear.

Fourteen years later, I ran into Dick Goodwin, one of Kennedy's speechwriters. I reminded him of my speech-writing contribution to the Kennedy campaign back in 1960.

"I'm the guy who wrote that stuff about a national fuels policy," I said.

Goodwin looked perplexed. "National fuels policy? Oh, yeah. *Hmmm* . . . we came out in *favor* of that, didn't we?"

How quickly they forget.

On another occasion, working for Selvage & Lee, I was assigned to Ghost-with-Cover on the Anderson windshield wiper company account. Old man Anderson, the Last of the Red Hot Individualists, had a hang-up about establishing a Federal Fair Trade bill.

Fair Trade is a PR euphemism for setting minimum prices on national brand merchandise. Discount houses around the country, who have their own PR operatives grinding out copy, were successful in giving Fair Trade a bad name. It became synonymous with Price-Fixing. So Anderson re-euphemized the legislation as the Quality Stabilization bill.

During the three months I worked on the account, I

pounded out 180 Senate and House floor speeches for the bill's proponents. Anderson's lapel-grabber in Washington relayed word back to Gary, Indiana, the Windshield Wiper Capital of the World, that he'd located a Stakhanovite of wordsmithing, a speechwritin' fool.

Quality Stabilization *née* Price-Fixing had unusual, across-the-board backing in Congress, from liberal Democrat to conservative Republican. This was because most Senators and Congressmen: (1) had plants in their states/ districts where national brand products were manufactured; or (2) were getting mail from old-line neighborhood druggists threatened by discount retailers.

It was hectic work. A call would come in at 10:00 A.M. to report that Hubert Humphrey, one of the bill's major supporters, was interested in a speech that day. I would draft it and ship it to the Hill by noon. Then pick up the Congressional Record next day to find that the particular speech I had crafted—if that's the word—for liberal Democrat Humphrey had actually been delivered by conservative Republican Dirksen, another supporter of Quality Stabilization.

"What happened?" I would ask old man Anderson's lapel-grabber when he called the next morning to put in that day's order.

"Hubert had to fly back to Minnesota so we just moved it over to Ev."

"Did he like it?" I would ask.

"Who cares?" the lobbyist would say. "He made it, so what the hell's the difference whether he liked it or not."

At other times, when a speech couldn't be "moved over" because the lapel-man couldn't locate another Senator or Congresman, sponsors of a bill would see that the material was stuck into the back part of the Congressional

Record as an "Extension of Remarks." For the cognoscenti of planting PR dross in the Record, this tells you that the stuff wasn't actually spoken on the floor of the Senate or House. But to the client living in Gary, Indiana, or Fort Worth, Texas, it's all the same.

Which, for those who may wonder how so much schlock gets into the Congressional Record, is why I ground out 180 speeches in three months. While, in another office building nearby, my opposite number in a rival PR agency was trying to keep up, funneling *his* dross to congressional friends of the retail discount industry.

They were all speeches written either not to be read or to be read to empty chambers. Why go to all that trouble when nobody is listening in Washington? Well, you take these tearsheets out of the Congressional Record, reprint tens of thousands of copies, and then mail the copies around the country to newspapers, women's clubs, or anybody who may take it seriously and give it a ride in an editorial or club publication.

Mail costs? Forget it. The Senator or Congressman who uses the material can move it out by frank. All the PR operator has to do is underwrite the cost of reprinting his own crap at the Government Printing Office, where a special rate is given to members of Congress.

All of which is known as developing grassroots support.

This was the kind of print deluge PR practiced by the Nixon White House. Chuck Colson's shop would write and plant pro-Administration speeches with friendly members of Congress, then reprint and whip the material around the country. The same practice was followed with friendly newspaper editorials, some White House-inspired.

It was while working the Quality Stabilization account that I pulled off my first Congressional Record Hat

Trick. Until then, I'd been able to make several Double Dips, but no Hat Trick.

A Double Dip consists of writing a speech for a Senator or Congressman to be delivered before an association convention, either in Washington or out of town. The association pays the speaker anywhere from $500 to $2,000 honorarium, plus travel and lodging expenses if the speech is on the road. In addition, so that his overworked staff doesn't have to worry over the minor detail of what their boss is going to say at the meeting, the association's PR shop furnishes him with a completed speech on an issue of interest to the association membership.

The Double Dip comes after the speech is made. You've written the speech. Now, to make sure your speaker knows how much your association client appreciates his taking time away from his busy schedule to fly out to Lake Tahoe and deliver a tailor-made speech for $2,000, you get his/your stirring words inserted into the Congressional Record by another friendly member of Congress. Then reprint, circulate, and stir until smooth and foamy.

The Hat Trick, the ultimate chutzpah that squeezes the last drop out of your client's honorarium, consists of doing the Double Dip—then, in another speech written for still a *third* friendly lawmaker, favorably quoting the first speech, e.g.:

> A few weeks ago, in an address before the American Council of Gastropoda Manufacturers, Senator Irving Klutz, my good friend and distinguished colleague, summed up this threat to the American free enterprise system. Said Senator Klutz . . .

So much for the fun part of Ghosting-with-Cover on behalf of industrial-commercial clients. The ulcers come

197

when the PR man has to draft material for the president of the association or company himself. Sure, you're good enough to ship drivel to Senators, Congressmen, even Presidential candidates. But can you really distill the *style* and *personality* of the client himself?

It's not too difficult on paper because American business leaders are given to speaking in bromides. They're all Short-Sentence Jerries.

True, from time to time you run into a business leader willing to risk a Learned Quote or two to establish an image as a Statesman of Industry. Every two years or so, *Fortune* introduces the waiting public to yet another PR manufactured quoter of T. S. Eliot or Origen. As if to say: "Look, folks, a businessman who can read." Robert McNamara was a prototype of this genre.

Fortunately, every business leader I ever worked for resisted my PR efforts to be converted into a Statesman of Industry. I say *fortunately*, because that's one con game I don't have on my conscience.

There is no such thing, you see, as a Statesman of Industry. Or for that matter, a Statesman of Labor. It's a term invented by public relations men to feed client egos: a myth perpetuated by *Fortune* magazine to justify Henry Luce's faith in the spirituality of money making.

All my business clients ever wanted, however, were variations on the Damn the Socialist Welfare State speech delivered by Secretary of Commerce Herbert Hoover, circa 1925.

It would have been a snap assignment if the clients had left the speechwriter to his own clichés. Except that clients invariably take their own dross more seriously than the stuff they pay you to ship up to Capitol Hill. Result: speechwriting-by-committee, one of God's subtle ways of punishing PR men for their sins of flesh, spirit, and verb.

So there I'd be in a conference room, surrounded by half a dozen assorted industry executives—$250 thousand in annual salaries tied up in one room for three to five hours to nit-pick a twenty-minute address to be delivered by the chairman of the board, a speech in which, among other things, he would savagely attack the Federal government for wasteful administrative practices.

One personality I'll always remember from those speechwriting conferences—there's one in every company and association—filled the role of Chief Nit-Picker. Usually he was the Vice President in Charge of Accounting, whose presence at the meeting was justified on grounds that he had "an ear for words." Sometimes the client's secretary would also be called in by the client because she "knows what I like."

The Chief Nit-Picker always had a giveaway phrase before he picked his first nit: "Let me," he would say after the client commented that the speech draft looked good, "Let me play the devil's advocate for a moment . . ."

Good-bye first draft. Back to the typewriter to mix the same clichés in different order. After which the Chief Nit-Picker, at Speech Conference No. 2, would nod approvingly and say: "Now *that* sounds more like *JC.*"

But while business clients paid the fattest fees (for an equal amount of Maalox), my greatest satisfaction as a speechwriter came when I had a chance to work for politicians who weren't afraid of sentences that ran longer than a dozen words. Too bad: there were only a few pols like that around.

One disappointment along this line came when I was canned as a speechwriter for "Sudden Death" Dole, a colorful, quick-witted public orator. That's Senator Robert Dole of Kansas, the former Republican party national chairman. He hired me to grind out headline-making speeches during his first campaign for the U.S. Senate.

I lasted four speeches with Dole before getting the ax. No disgrace there, because up to that time writing four consecutive speeches for "Sudden Death" Dole before being terminated was a record (since broken by Lyn Nofziger, who in 1971 actually ran off seven in a row).

Dole's hired speechwriting hands always had a tough time because the Kansas Senator demanded—in addition to brilliant, orgiastic texts—a ton of accompanying publicity.

Since publicity beyond the speaking site is 75 percent of the reason a politician makes a campaign appearance, Dole's demand wasn't unreasonable. What was unreasonable was that he expected his writers to come up with a headline *every* speech. The argument that Babe Ruth struck out occasionally carried no weight with "Sudden Death." It was a case of publish or perish.

Well, Mom, I tried. Honest I did. But pressing for headlines with every public utterance is a dangerous exercise in PR brinksmanship. The best way to get a headline, as anybody who reads knows, is to attack something. To get a headline the next day, you have to attack something *harder*. Same each succeeding day. By the fourth day, you're reaching, you see. And there comes trouble, right there in River City. Or was it Wichita?

On the fourth day, following a campus riot somewhere, I handed Dole a speech quoting J. Edgar Hoover, the All-Venerated, to the effect that some of those campus demonstrations were Communist-inspired. Dole read the Venerated Quote, then woke up the following morning to find his name in not one but *two* headlines. The first report covered the speech; the second, in an editorial in some small town paper, denounced him for "neo-Mc-Carthyism."

"You got me *touched up* there, buddy," Dole smiled, pulling the arrow out of his rib cage.

"We were quoting *Hoover*, Bob," I tried to explain. "J. Edgar or Herbert, how much safer can you get in Kansas?"

Much, much safer. He paid me off on the spot. They didn't call him "Sudden Death" for nothing.

Hyper-sensitivity to media criticism for something contained in a text wasn't one of the difficulties a speech-writer ran into working for Spiro Agnew. While the former Vice President was thin-skinned about press coverage generally, criticism that resulted from anything he uttered in a public speech didn't faze him. He actually seemed to enjoy it at times.

"They'll climb walls at *The Washington Post* when they hear this," Agnew would exult, going over a speech draft he especially liked. Of his pet hates in the print press, *The Washington Post* remained the one he most loved to hate. This was because of an editorial that paper ran when Agnew was first selected by Nixon as a Vice Presidential running mate in 1968. It compared Nixon's selection of the then Maryland Governor to Caligula's choice of his horse as Roman proconsul.

Agnew never forgave Kay Graham or her newspaper for that affront. Every effort to get the Vice President together with *Post* editors for a let's-kiss-and-make-up editorial board conference was turned off. Far from being jumpy about an unfavorable editorial comment by the *Post*, Agnew savored it.

Agnew's meteoric rise as a public speaker after becoming Vice President wasn't, as some believed, a matter of either accident or White House contrivance. No politician in America worked harder preparing for a speech.

Technically, Agnew wasn't a gifted orator. His style of delivery was flat and atonal. But he had, if not charisma (a word he despised), a certain stage presence. His penchant for detail extended to mike placement, voice modulation, phrasing, breath control, and eye contact. Agnew spent rehearsal time on every aspect of every speech appearance.

"Where are the cheer lines?" he'd ask after looking over a dull speech draft. "I don't see any cheer lines."

Then he'd write some in himself. His best remembered phrase—"effete corps of impudent snobs"—was, in fact, written that way, after he reviewed a well-constructed but publicity-dry speech on ICBM and MIRV military capabilities.

Writing speeches for Agnew was a regimen. He required drafts on his desk forty-eight to seventy-two hours ahead of delivery. Then he would go over the material word by word, altering and rewriting. And he rarely delivered a draft in its original form. The most memorable exception was Pat Buchanan's speech attacking the television news media, delivered at Des Moines in November, 1969, at White House suggestion.

At times, when a particularly good speech draft was submitted, Agnew would grade it "A-plus" or "A," sending it back to the writer with a scrawled comment, "Excellent." Once, for a speech attacking B. F. Skinner's book, *Beyond Freedom and Dignity*, Herb Thompson was graded "Magnificent."

Unfortunately, the Skinner speech itself got little substantive news coverage on television because of another Agnew penchant—one which I, as his press secretary, could only grimace-and-bear. After sweating over speech drafts, he'd always call for half a dozen warm-up gags, which he edited with the same meticulous care taken on the speech itself.

"Audience-warmers," he would explain.

The business of hiring professional gag writers to loosen up audiences was another Kennedy contribution to modern-day political speechmaking. After Stevenson broke the humor barrier, professionals moved in. By the mid-1960s, every major national politician—including conservatives like Barry Goldwater—was reading one-liners crafted by some top West Coast gagwriting pro.

One of the first people Short-Sentence Jerry Ford put on his speechwriting payroll after becoming Vice President was a professional gag writer. Agnew's pro was Ray Siller, out of Los Angeles. But at one time or another, every member of the traveling staff pitched in with topical gags to keep the boss happy. Once, at an Army-Navy Benefit in Los Angeles, the Vice President preceded Bob Hope at the microphone. Hope, sitting next to his nephew and Agnew's traveling aide, Peter Malatesta, grumbled and crossed out joke after joke from his own prepared one-liners because the Vice President was using the same topical material.

"Who the hell is writing this guy's stuff?" Hope finally demanded of his nephew. Malatesta told him it was Ray Siller. Hope ended up hiring the gag writer as a member of his own staff.

From a PR perspective, the problem with Agnew's penchant for warm-up jokes was that they were perfectly suited to fit into a one- to three-minute segment of television news. This meant that the following morning the Vice President would turn on the *Today* show and catch a series of his one-liners, but no coverage of the body of the speech itself.

He'd call me in to complain: this obviously was a conspiracy of the goddamned networks, he'd say. Next time out I'd remind him of the problem, cautioning that if he overdid the gag material, he'd upstage his own show.

But it was no use. The one-liners stayed in, and in time, I learned to accept this as a fact of life as Spiro Agnew's press secretary.

So the man I worked for was a frustrated stand-up comic? Things could be worse, I would remind myself. I was lucky. But for the grace of the PR gods, I might have ended up writing speeches for Short-Sentence Jerry Ford.

11. Silver Anvils, Clay Feet

The conscious and intelligent manipulation of the organized habits and opinions of the masses is an important element in democratic society.

Edward Bernays, *Propaganda*

Every spring, the Sons & Daughters of Edward Bernays and Ivy Lee, operating under the aegis of the Public Relations Society of America, come together at a lavish dinner in the Grand Ballroom of the Waldorf-Astoria to pat themselves on the back and distribute their professional Oscars.

Called Silver Anvils—*"Good public relations is forged through public opinion."*—dozens of glistening trophies are awarded to PR agencies and practitioners. In recent years, however, these Silver Anvils, coveted as they are by PR professionals, have come to represent something less than the best.

Not that PRSA's award-winning programs don't strike all the right anvil chords by Establishment standards. It's just that the most effective "manipulation of the organized habits and opinions of the masses" carried on these days is the work of anti-Establishmentarians.

At some point in the early 1960s—about the time *Unsafe at Any Speed* was going into galley proofs—the propaganda efforts of Establishment PR pros like Selvage & Lee and Hill & Knowlton began to come up short when measured alongside those of a new breed of dedicated non-professional activists.

In fact, by Bernays' classic definition, Ralph Nader is probably the best PR practitioner in the business today. Except, of course, he isn't in the business. Which is why Mr. Consumer Advocate, operating through his own foundation-supported activist groups, has made more impact on American habits and opinions than all the PRSA Silver Anvil winners put together.

Most PR pros argue that Nader's publicity success working against their clients is due to a liberal media's affinity for what he's selling on the idea market. That may be true in part, but as I see it from the perspective of a decade and a half on the PR frontlines, there's a far more fundamental reason.

No matter how much they may protest otherwise, you see, the Sons & Daughters of Bernays-Lee are mercenaries. Sure, they're dedicated, but if a client drops the agency, the PR pro working the account just picks up his skills and moves off to the next propaganda battle. Provided, of course, that the fee is big enough to support his dedication in the style to which it's accustomed.

The true activist advocate, on the other hand, is motivated by stirrings in the viscus rather than the bank account. As a result, he has hold of the most "important element" of all in any contest of human ideas: the element of credibility.

And that, I guess, is also the reason why the propaganda campaign I'll probably be best remembered for is the one I took on some eight months after leaving the Vice President's office and quitting the field of professional public relations.

True, it was a campaign built on quicksand. But until the moment Spiro Agnew resigned his office and pleaded *nolo contendere* in return for a suspended sentence, my advocacy of his innocence for eight hectic Indian summer weeks had been a labor of faith.

I believed in Agnew's innocence for reasons which, even now, make more sense than the truth. Though I respected and liked the man, I knew he had his flaws. He could be vain, arrogant, insensitive, self-indulgent, and petulant. But never, I thought, devious. And never, despite what his political opposition may have thought, stupid.

It just didn't add up. Not at all. Of all the venal asses who've held the job and stayed out of the coils, why would Spiro Agnew be the first governor of Maryland to get caught, like that Louisiana governor of my youth?

No, all that made sense to me at that time was that the Nixon White House, sinking slowly into its Watergate wallow, had somehow instigated the Agnew investigation in order to take the heat off No. 1. One day the country was reading nothing but Watergate; the next day, nothing but Agnew. I knew Hertz' *modus operandi*. If ever I smelled a dirty trick operation, this was it.

So for two months, operating on that belief, I ran a one-man propaganda office, arguing my former client's case in the court of public opinion. No leak sprung by the White House staff or the prosecutors went unanswered. My professional neck was on the line—I'd just signed up to do a nationally-syndicated column—but for all the risk involved, calling Elliot Richardson a pompous Boston Brahmin had its psychological compensation.

Through all this, I contacted Agnew only at two crucial points. First, to ask whether he wanted me to shut up. The word came back: No. Second, to ask whether there was anything to rumors that he was plea bargaining and might resign. The word came back: No.

Then, at 2:05 P.M., October 10, Spiro Agnew walked into the Federal District Building in Baltimore and proved to be, like those PRSA Silver Anvils, something less than advertised. He called me two days later to thank me for what I'd done on his behalf. There were, he said, reasons . . .

I told him I understood. But the truth is, like millions of others who also believed, I'm still trying.

I left my job as Spiro Agnew's press secretary in mid-January, 1973, just before the second Nixon-Agnew Inauguration. Watergate was then only a myth concocted by *The Washington Post.* Agnew was at the top of his world, a paragon of Middle American virtue and heir-apparent to the 1976 Republican Presidential nomination.

So why leave a politician when he's at the top? For the same reason Vic Schiro gave when asked why he announced plans for the Superdome two days before an election: Can you think of a better time?

Leaving after a landslide victory—when all your political indicators are up and your client doesn't need you—is the only way to go. Not that it was easy.

After two and a half years, I'd come to enjoy the perqs and privileges that go with the life-style of Washington power at its highest level. For at least a month after they took my private White House Signal phone out of our house—the line that can put a Presidential or Vice Presidential staff man in touch with anyone in the world, just by lifting the receiver and saying, "I want to talk to . . ."—I suffered power-withdrawal bends.

Getting tickets to New York shows at the last minute became harder when the call was coming from Vic Gold rather than Vic Gold, *press secretary to the Vice President.* Predictably, the invitations to Washington parties fell off. In Hollywood East, it's not so much what-have-you-done-for-me-lately as what-can-you-do-for-me-tomorrow.

But sooner or later it had to happen. I'd come to a decision that I was going to leave Spiro Agnew's employ because, after a decade and a half as an upwardly mobile political hack, I discovered that I really didn't want what I thought I wanted when I came to Washington.

Why not? Re-read the preceding sentence for clues. Specifically, seven uses of the first person singular but only one reference to Spiro Agnew. It's what those sticklers about White House staff anonymity and Loyalty, with a capital "L," would call a conflict of interest.

The greatest praise I ever heard given a White House aide—at least, judging from the breathless tone in which it was said—was that he was "so Loyal to the Old Man he'd walk out a twenty-fifth-story window without asking why."

Before he finally left the White House, Ron Ziegler, the staff man who rated that encomium, had in the name of "Loyalty," done just about everything else for "the Old Man."

All right, put it down to acrophobia or curiosity. But for one reason or another, I couldn't be that *Loyal.* Even if I managed a blindfold to cure my fear of heights, there would always be that nagging need to know, just before the plunge into the White House press room: *Why this trip?*

And so, one afternoon in October, 1972, at age forty-four, I'd made up my mind that for all the perquisites of the job of press secretary to a Vice President or President, there had to be better ways to pay my social and political dues than to live as a human satellite orbiting a major planet.

It was that simple. I was going to leave the field of professional PR in order to do whatever conscious, intelligent manipulating the world needed, on my *own* rather than someone else's terms. I had had it with the Great Myth self-indulged by PR pros everywhere, from Bernays to the present day, that they, not the people they work for, are the major planets in the power constellation.

Not that the PR pro can't serve a useful satellite function. But he's more technician than manipulator. And not necessarily the most important technician around, either.

Gene McCarthy put it all in perspective during the Wisconsin Presidential primary of 1968. One morning McCarthy's traveling press secretary, in a fit of professional rage, dis-Loyally packed his bags and left. A reporter asked the candidate whether the defection might damage his campaign.

"Not at all," McCarthy replied without hesitation. "Losing a press secretary can't hurt a campaign. But, now, if I were to lose my *driver* . . ."

My last day on the job as Spiro Agnew's press secretary was January 15, 1973. Let the record show that on the morning of January 16, the Vice President of the United States was picked up by Gus Holmes, his driver, and taken to work. On schedule, as usual.

> *"Kim Novak? If you wanna bring me your wife or your aunt, we'll do the same for them."*
>
> Producer Harry Cohn on the Making of a Superstar, Hollywood West

Excerpt from an AP dispatch, June, 1974:
New York (AP)—For $9,600, Madison Avenue offers a two-day course for eight in how to deal with the news media, and plans to begin offering a similar program on how to act before a congressional committee.

J. Walter Thompson, one of the nation's largest advertising and public relations firms, offers executives a two-day telecommunications development course from former television newsman Sander Vanocur and other broadcasting journalists.

The corporate chiefs learn how to dress and act on camera, how to defuse potentially damaging questions and how to cope with aggressive interviewers . . .

Give me your tired, your wretched (but not your poor!), says the PR pro, and with modern technology and my expertise, all things are possible. Like Harry Cohn in Hollywood West, I can do the same for you, your wife or your aunt, in Hollywood East.

You're a business klutz and wanna handle a congressional committee? Tell ya what I'm gonna do. Get seven of your friends together and for $4,800 a day . . .

You're a political klutz and wanna be President? Well, for that I charge a little more.

And so, the Great American PR Myth goes on, promising feats of imagectomy for those who believe that all it takes to manipulate the organized habits and opinions of the masses is (1) cosmetics, and (2) technique.

Such was the faith of the Nixon White House, that a

President who had grown up and was immersed in the myth thought he could handle a criminal conspiracy as "a little PR problem." And like Shakespeare's Macbeth, Richard Nixon was betrayed in the end by his delusion. He was convinced that PR magic—especially incantations into a TV camera—could cosmetize and cover up a massive political crime. But then again, maybe the former President was misled by the rave reviews he got over the years for his alleged skills as a PR manipulator.

For example, there was Joe McGinniss' *Selling of the President, 1968*. That book was a bonanza to political PR agencies looking for business. It did more than a thousand promo flyers to enhance the myth that there's a winning PR formula to control every political situation or elect any candidate.

Does the myth have substance? Can political man live by PR alone? Could the American people be "sold" a President—in the memorable phrase of one of Nelson Rockefeller's Madison Avenue PR aides—"like so much Alka-Seltzer"?

PR pros like Clif White, Joe Napolitan, Mark Shields, and Lyn Nofziger argue yes. Cynical journalists like McGinniss back them up. But after a decade and a half in the PR business—working campaigns from local tax assessor to President—I've come to some different conclusions, such as: (1) you can't sell Alka-Seltzer in a Bromo Seltzer market; and (2) you can't sell *either* when you're working with a candidate who hasn't got anything more to offer than political fizz.

There's no question, in a media-saturated society, that PR techniques are here to stay. They *may* even have a legitimate role to play in the democratic process. Somebody has to tell political klutzes to wear blue shirts for the

TV cameras (but not brown shoes with a blue suit to a Southhampton fund-raiser).

Still, if PR alone could sell the people in a democratic society something they wouldn't otherwise buy, then John Lindsay—who was *born* knowing everything Sander Vanocur will teach you and seven of your friends for $4,800 a day—should have run off with the Democratic nomination in 1972.

And what about Hubert Humphrey? While McGinniss was doing his inside job on the 1968 Nixon campaign, Humphrey, under Napolitan's expert PR hand, was *losing* with the same techniques—right down to the identical shade of TV pancake make-up.

For that matter, what about the Alka-Seltzerizing of Nelson Rockefeller, the man who's done more to subsidize the PR/advertising business in the past fifteen years than any rival political institution in the Western world? If PR can make a President, how did it happen that in 1964 Rockefeller lost the Republican nomination to the original *anti*-PR candidate, Barry Goldwater?

The standard PR answer to that one is that Rockefeller's divorce-and-remarriage was an insurmountable obstacle even his experts could not overcome. Which is an accurate answer, as far as it goes. But it doesn't explain why Rockefeller's PR salesmen couldn't move public opinion on the divorce-and-remarriage issue in 1964, when a decade later it's a fact of political change-of-life.

Governor Marvin Mandel of Maryland, for example, last year left his wife of three decades to marry a divorcee. Yet he was re-elected by an overwhelming vote in a state with a large Catholic (and menopause) vote. Mandel is no exception, either. He's only the latest (at least, at this writing) of a growing number of Governors, Senators, and

Congressmen who've switched marriage partners and survived at the polls, despite an old political PR wives' tale that it can't be done.

In fact, if Rockefeller or any other divorced-and-remarried candidate were to run for President in 1976, the insurmountable obstacle of the 1964 race would hardly be a factor. True, it would lose some fringe votes. But no more than, say, a Catholic candidate for President might lose from another end of the political spectrum. (Remember when that, too, was a political no-no? You couldn't run a Catholic, see, because back in 1928 . . .)

Quite a change in "the organized habits and opinions of the masses"—all in a brief period of time. And what did PRSA's Silver Anvil winners and the PR fizz hucksters of the political world have to do with bringing about this change? Absolutely nothing.

On the contrary, in one of the most dynamic eras of cultural and political transition in our country's history, the role of the PR professional, attached to his Establishment base, has been that of reacting to, rather than manipulating, swift moving events.

In my fifteen years as a PR pro, American society witnessed: (1) a black revolution, (2) a consumer revolution, (3) a youth revolution, and (4) a revolution in attitudes toward women and sex. Separately and together these revolutions triggered a massive movement away from customs and traditions that had existed for centuries.

And what were Vic Gold and his expert fellow manipulators doing while all this was going on? Dreaming up shticks for the grand opening of Howard Johnson Motor Lodges. Trying to push political candidates on the open market "like so much Alka-Seltzer."

What manipulative wonders we've witnessed in our time, you see, have been the product not of our PR pros but of men and women, young and old, working from the grassroots level rather than the rarefied atmosphere of the board room. Propagandists for causes in which they believed.

The kind of propagandists, that is, who didn't need a two-day $9,600 course given by J. Walter Thompson counseling them on "how to deal with the news media . . . how to dress and act on camera . . . how to cope with aggressive interviewers."

J. Walter Thompson, remember? If you don't, let me refresh your memory. They're the same wonderful experts who gave us Ron Ziegler and H. R. Haldeman.

12. Night of Tri u m p h: II

> *You have helped make our last campaign our best campaign of all. Now let us make the next four years the best four years in American history.*
>
> Richard Nixon, November 7, 1972

———◆———

Aboard the *Titanic* not long before it struck the iceberg . . .

"Four years from now," Spiro Agnew's lifelong friend Bud Hammerman was telling anybody who'd stand still long enough to listen, "four years from now it'll be Ted against Teddy. You think *this* celebration's something? Four years from now . . ."

Six months from then, A. H. (Bud) Hammerman II, Spiro Agnew's old friend and political associate would go before a Baltimore grand jury to seal the Federal government's case against his candidate for President in 1976.

Election night, 1972, Hammerman's seemed the only exultant voice in an oddly restrained Vice Presidential victory suite at the Shoreham Hotel. Scripted victories are like that. There were no whoops, no hugs and kisses for the cameras, not even a raised voice.

All of that had been left downstairs, in the tumult of the grand ballroom. After Nixon's speech and departure,

Agnew's official schedule for the evening called for only a visit to a fatcat contributors' party elsewhere in the hotel. When he returned to the suite, the Vice President moved quietly among clusters of his guests—close personal friends from the old Baltimore days (like Hammerman), a few celebrities (Frank Sinatra, Sammy Davis, Jr.), staff aides, and their families.

In the background, unheeded, the voices of the networks' instant analysts droned on, reporting on what we knew, as early as 10 P.M., would be the greatest Presidential landslide in American history.

By 1:00 A.M., the Vice Presidential suite was practically cleared. Dale and I woke our kids, clustered in beds in an adjoining room, said our good-byes to Spiro and Judy Agnew one last time, and left.

The route from the Shoreham to our home in northern Virginia, by way of Theodore Roosevelt Bridge, takes you down Rock Creek Parkway, then left onto Virginia Avenue. The Washington Monument lies six blocks straight ahead—optically enlarged, like the full moon on the horizon. On the right, the Watergate office- and apartment-complex; on the left, directly across from the Watergate, the Howard Johnson Motor Lodge that Howard Hunt used as a look-out site on the night of the Watergate break-in.

Opening the Virginia Avenue Howard Johnson with a publicity bang had been one of my PR assignments back when I was handling the Washington end of the account for Selvage & Lee. We'd been retained to publicize Hojo's new motor lodge chain along the East Coast. Someone suggested we take-a-ride on the Bobby Kennedy hiking craze then going on. Get a bunch of college kids to hike from Manhattan to Virginia Avenue, stopping at a Hojo lodge every night.

Three kids made the hike, 250 miles from midtown Manhattan to Washington, D.C. They arrived in Washington late one afternoon, first coming into TV camera range on the stretch of open ground along the Potomac where the Watergate would be built a few years later.

As they straggled up to the new motor lodge entrance, I handed the lead hiker a pair of scissors. According to script, he cut a Hojo-colored orange ribbon stretched across the entrance driveway. Then someone stuck a microphone in his face. How did he feel? According to script, he was supposed to say: Great. Staying at all those Hojo lodges had kept him and his friends fresh enough to go out for a night on the town.

Instead, soaking his feet in a pan of hot water, what he said was: "How do I feel? Stupid. What the hell did it prove?"

We got lucky. A freedom bus was stoned in Alabama that same afternoon, and our grand opening film footage ended up on the newsroom floor.

Still, I didn't hold it against the kid. He had a point. I couldn't answer him then, and I still can't.

If I could, I'd have stayed in the PR business, wouldn't I?